The Inward Path *to* God

A Prayer Journey
with
St. Teresa of Ávila

Wayne Simsic

The Inward Path *to* God

A Prayer Journey
with
St. Teresa of Ávila

Wayne Simsic

Published by The Word Among Us Press
7115 Guilford Drive, Suite 100
Frederick, Maryland 21704
www.wau.org

19 18 17 16 15   1 2 3 4 5

ISBN: 978-1-59325-270-0
eISBN: 978-1-59325-465-0

Cover design by Koechel Peterson & Associates

Unless otherwise noted, Scripture citations are from the New Jerusalem Bible, copyright © 1985 by Darton, Longman, & Todd, Ltd., and Doubleday, a division of Bantam Doubleday Dell Publishing Group, Inc. Reprinted by permission.

All references to the writings of St. Teresa of Ávila except for the poetry are taken from *The Collected Works of St. Teresa of Avila*, Volume One and Two, translated by Kieran Kavanaugh and Otilio Rodriguez. Volume One: *The Book of Her Life, Spiritual Testimonies, Soliloquies,* copyright © 1976. Volume Two: *The Way of Perfection, The Interior Castle,* copyright © 1980. Both by the Washington Province of Discalced Carmelites, ICS Publications, 2131 Lincoln Road, NE, Washington, DC 2002-1199, www.icspublications.org. Reprinted by permission.

Poetry references are taken from *The Complete Poetry of St. Teresa of Avila,* trans. Eric W. Vogt, University Press of the South, 1996.

Made and printed in the United States of America

Library of Congress Control Number: 2014955768

To my mother and father

ACKNOWLEDGMENTS

This book evolved out of a personal need to explore Teresa of Ávila's call to pray more deeply and more contemplatively for seekers today. Its pages are filled with the voices of participants in seminars and retreats who, through the years, eagerly offered their heartfelt enthusiasm for Teresa's wise guidance in their lives.

In the preparation of this book, I have received support and critical feedback from many. I am grateful to Sr. Mercia Madigan, Casey Toohig, Joseph Geiger, and Sue Allen for their careful reading of the text and their willingness to share their personal insights. Their interest was both encouraging and helpful. I also want to thank Patricia Mitchell, my editor, who welcomed and supported this project. My wife, Diana, remained encouraging and life-giving throughout the process, consistently reinforcing my vision with her enthusiasm.

I owe a special word of thanks to the Carmelites who, through their ministry and scholarship, have greatly enriched my life and have been a source of inspiration for so many seeking support for their contemplative path.

Finally, to my mother and father, who were a grace to me in ways they may never have suspected, I dedicate this book with gratitude and love.

TABLE OF CONTENTS

Abbreviations Used in This Book

IC: *The Interior Castle*

WP: *The Way of Perfection*

BL: *The Book of Her Life*

F: *Foundations*

P: *Poetry*

T: *Spiritual Testimonies*

Teresa: A Guide for the Journey

*Do not be frightened . . . by the many things
you need to consider in order to begin this divine journey
which is the royal road to heaven. A great treasure is
gained by traveling this road; no wonder we have
to pay what seems to us a high price.*

—*The Way of Perfection, 21.1*

During a conversation with a small group about the mystics who influence our lives, I mentioned how much I admire Teresa of Ávila's pragmatic, down-to-earth approach to prayer and spirituality. A middle-aged man added that for years he has used Teresa's writings, particularly *The Way of Perfection,* as a source of inspiration for his prayer life. What caught my attention was the long history of his relationship with Teresa as a spiritual guide. A young woman chimed in and talked so freely and warmly about Teresa's importance to her as a mentor that I found myself imagining the saint standing alongside her and smiling.

Listening to this exchange, it was clear to me that even though she lived in the sixteenth century and in a culture much different from our own, Teresa's words and wisdom have the power to leap across the barrier of gender, time, and culture. In her masterpiece *The Interior Castle,* she advises that we should look to the lives of the saints for consolation and encouragement. She writes, "It's necessary that we speak to, think about, and become the companions of those who having had a mortal body accomplished such great feats for God" (IC VI.7.6). Perhaps we should take her at her word and begin our own personal dialogue with her.

Her gift is not only that she reveals her struggle and human weakness in opening herself to God's grace, but also that she shares her journey with others. Readers identify with her because she discovered God despite all her frailty and resistance. She was not afraid to admit difficulty with prayer and discouragement with mental distractions.

Though she was given an extraordinary gift of visions and ecstatic experiences, there is a humanity and an authenticity about Teresa that captures the imagination and makes her accessible to us today. She had a deep need for relationships throughout her life and treasured the love and friendship that she cultivated with John of the Cross, Peter of Alcantara, Jerome Gracían, and a number of Jesuit confessors, among others. Her many letters are filled with wit and humor, and sometimes impatience and anger, but they always reveal a person interested in honest human contact. "You must forgive me," she wrote to a friend she had hurt. "With those I love I am insufferable, so anxious am I to have them perfect in everything."[1]

Teresa allays our fear that holiness will take away the uniqueness of our personality and remove us from those we love. Despite her growth in prayer and her lifelong process of transformation, she did not lose her warmhearted personality, her sense of humor, or her commonsense, practical tendencies. She simply worked hard, enjoyed life, and continued to find pleasure in it even to the end. Nor did her holiness distance her from others but, in fact, made her more vulnerable in her relationships.

Teresa's passion for God and radical dedication to this deepest truth of her life can call us to set out on our own prayer journey with her as a guide. She shows us that intimacy with God is possible, and that if we are willing to forget ourselves, we can fall in love with him beyond our wildest imaginings.

Her zeal for God propelled her along the labyrinthine paths of an "inner castle" where she learned to walk humbly in the company of Christ. She challenges us to be true to our own journey and to ask ourselves, "What is the passion in my own life? Is it hidden or buried under layers of concern and fear? How can I uncover my desire to set out on a spiritual adventure?"

Though Teresa was in continual communication with God as with a friend, it would be foolish to assume that this intimacy was cozy or predictable, or that Teresa herself was above complaining to God about his seemingly harsh treatment. It is said that once when Teresa was pleading to God for help in establishing a convent, she heard this reply: "I heard you; let Me alone."[2]

One caveat: Teresa, like all the saints, followed the gospel path with abandon. She warns us that authentic love calls for sacrifice, and the highest expression of it will always entail a complete self-offering. We cannot follow a path toward divine intimacy without being willing to pay the cost. Teresa understood that even with the best intentions, "we are so miserly and so slow in giving ourselves entirely to God" (BL 11.1). Following Christ has never been easy, and unless we are interested in getting hopelessly lost, Teresa knew that we must walk the path that he did, which includes the cross. She assures us, though, that any effort we put forth will be rewarded abundantly. We only need to participate in the best way we can and leave the rest up to God.

Speaking from Experience

I shall say nothing about what I have not experienced myself . . .
[or received understanding of from our Lord in prayer.]
(The Way of Perfection, Prologue, 3)

One of the primary reasons, I believe, that Teresa attracts us as a spiritual guide is her personal approach to the inner journey. Her willingness to share her experience appeals to our desire today to explore our own experience of God. We want to know how someone discovers God and finds interior peace, particularly as this unfolds in the uniqueness of one's own personal history.

When I use the word "experience," I am not referring to phenomena that sometimes occurred in Teresa's life, such as ecstasies, raptures, visions, and locutions. She considered these secondary and not essential for faith development. She was primarily concerned with the normal maturation of the life of grace and the practice of virtue. As baptized Christians, we can experience the same reality as Teresa but in a different way. One of Teresa's gifts is that she has the ability to wake us up so that we can claim the grace that is already at work in our lives.

All of Teresa's major writings, including the more formal *The Interior Castle*, flow from her experience of God and, as a result, communicate the depth of her spiritual path. Identifying with her words allows us to enter her experience and be influenced by it. Her writings, then, are direct conduits to our hearts: they do not simply tell us about God but immerse us in the mystery of divine love.

At first I found myself impatient with her writing style because she often moves away from the subject or even loses track of it altogether, only to return apologetically some time later. Then I imagined that she was a friend sharing spiritual guidance with me in the form of a letter, in the same way that she had counseled her fellow nuns. As a result, I not only became more patient with the text but found myself engaging the spirit of Teresa, identifying with her trials and joys in a personal way, which is often the case with live conversation.

You only have to read her colloquial style of writing to get the sense that she is sitting across from you and, like a true friend, takes to heart your spiritual welfare and offers counsel from her personal experience. Replying to a layman's concern about feeling sadness or melancholy during prayer, Teresa offers simple but wise advice:

> Take no notice of that feeling you get of wanting to leave off in the middle of your prayer, but praise the Lord for the desire you have to pray. . . . Try occasionally, when you find yourself oppressed . . . , to go to some place where you can see the sky, and walk up and down a little: doing that will not interfere with your prayer. . . . We are seeking God all the time, and it is because of this that we go about in search of means to that end, and it is essential that the soul should be led gently.[3]

Teresa's story had a dramatic impact on the lives of renowned figures such as Edith Stein and Dorothy Day. Before her conversion, Edith inadvertently picked up a copy of Teresa's autobiography and finished it in one night. Her response after completing the book? "This is the truth!"[4] Imagine how Edith must have felt. She was a philosopher who had been seeking truth mostly through rational discourse and then, profoundly moved by the experience of Teresa, came to realize the validity of an entirely different path, one focused predominantly on passion and love for God.

Dorothy Day, before her conversion, came to Teresa by way of William James' classic *The Varieties of Religious Experience*, which highlights the relationship between prayer and action in the saint's life. This example spoke to a deep desire in Dorothy to merge her involvement in social issues with her spiritual life. In her autobiography *The Long Loneliness*, Dorothy discusses how deeply the saint's humanity resonated with her:

> I had read the life of St. Teresa of Ávila and fallen in love with her. . . . Once when she was trying to avoid that recreation hour which is set aside in convents for nuns to be together, the others insisted on her joining them, and she took castanets and danced. When some older nuns professed themselves shocked, she retorted, "One must do things sometimes to make life more bearable."[5]

Later, when Dorothy was establishing her vision of the Catholic Worker and looking for guidance, she found support in Teresa's *Foundations,* which tells the story of how the saint answered the call to establish the first reformed Carmelite monastery.

Many today are looking for the authentic experience of those who have a wholehearted commitment to a life of prayer. Teresa shows us that such a commitment is possible and offers us her wisdom—wisdom gleaned not only from her own experience, but tested against the counsel of spiritual advisors (some more helpful than others), the tradition of the Church, and the Scriptures.

However, it is one thing to tell your story when there are no cultural restrictions and quite another when, as a woman, your words are being parsed by the Inquisition in Counter-Reformation Spain. The Inquisition was threatened enough by Teresa's autobiography to hold on to it for thirteen years. Women were commonly viewed as neither sophisticated or learned enough to write or preach about prayer. Women religious, in particular, were expected to limit themselves to practicing their faith through liturgy, works of mercy, and vocal prayer. They were not to explore the hidden terrain of the soul because "it's not for women, for they will be susceptible to illusions" (WP 21.2).

Even as a woman without a background in the theological thought of her day, Teresa found through prayer the strength and courage to raise her voice. Writing under obedience to her superiors, her writings nevertheless assured women of their dignity in the loving eyes of God and the potential of their relationship with Christ. She was never interested in isolating herself from the Church or her religious community. She wrote using the tone and assuming the role of a woman of the day, thus avoiding the scrutiny of academics. But she spoke with passion about the concerns that ruled her heart, cultivating her voice at a time when women feared raising their voices to publicly give witness to the truth. However, she saw herself not as a woman with unusual courage and fortitude but simply as a mouthpiece for God. All her inner wisdom arose from her fidelity to prayer.

PRACTICING PRAYER

I say that if these learned men do not practice prayer
their learning is of little help to beginners.
(The Book of Her Life, 13.16)

When it comes to her main concern, prayer, Teresa urged both beginners and those who guided them not to talk about prayer or read about it but to pray. She understood how difficult it is to pray but insisted that we must pray. We must *experience* God, not simply have knowledge *about* God.

Our knowledge of prayer may be extensive, but we may be insecure when it comes to our own prayer life. Wading into the water is one thing, but taking the risk and diving into the deep end is another thing altogether. For this reason, it may be difficult to read Teresa's writings because she calls us to face the truth revealed in prayer: that the divine presence is the reality of our lives, and all else is secondary. She emphasizes again and again: if you are not praying, begin to pray now; do not wait. If you cannot pray, then pray for the gift of prayer.

Because Teresa considered prayer not primarily a formal responsibility or an external act but a response to the rhythm of the Spirit, she emphasized the necessity of remaining open to God's presence, not only at certain times, but in the midst of daily life. Prayer is life itself. Her own passion for this Presence catapulted her into the depths of her being, bringing her wholeness and freedom. Not surprisingly, this movement inward gathered together all the frayed edges of her personality into greater self-knowledge and an all-consuming longing for the Beloved. This is the journey she shares with all those who will listen.

Teresa's dedication to prayer may remind us of the depth and mystery we have been ignoring in our own life. We recall what we too easily forget: our own longing for divine love. With an extraordinary humanness originating in her own experience of trials and joys, she coaxes us toward a commitment to something greater than ourselves.

More important, her guidance never seems harsh or forced but gentle and respectful of the uniqueness of each person's path: "It is important to understand that God doesn't lead all by one path, and perhaps the one who thinks she is walking along a very lowly path is in fact higher in the eyes of the Lord" (WP 17.2). Her principal concern? Our openness to the gift of contemplative prayer and ultimate union with divine love.

I am convinced that if a contemporary seeker reads Teresa with an open heart, he or she will be drawn in by the wisdom and humanness of a saint who not only shares the path with us but, like her companion St. John of the Cross, has a deep desire to teach others what it means to be a person of prayer. In my own journey, I have found in Teresa a perfect counterpart to the guidance of John of the Cross. Whereas John represents a laser-like focus inward expressed brilliantly in poetry and theological discourse, Teresa's path inward is complemented by an extraversion and a poetic imagination that fully engages the world around her and is firmly rooted in her story. Both, however, have left me with the same impression: the journey is worth the sacrifice.

Who Was Teresa?

Even though we know better and have been warned against it many times, it is easy to idealize a saint and place her or him on a pedestal. As a result, instead of becoming a guide for our own human struggle and our desire for holiness, the saint remains an abstraction removed from us by an unattainable sanctity.

Let us take this opportunity, then, to place Teresa's life in an historical context and explore her personal history.

Childhood

Teresa was born in the Castilian town of Ávila in 1515. At the time of her birth, the Renaissance was in full flower and the Reformation was gathering steam.

Ávila was not exactly a sleepy town. It had a strong military tradition, producing soldiers and leaders for battlefields throughout Europe, North Africa, and the New World. Out of her nine brothers, seven sailed with conquistadors and four were killed fighting in the New World. In Teresa's lifetime, Ávila also became a walled fortress in a long and bitter battle with the Moors. It is no surprise, then, that Teresa felt comfortable enough with martial imagery to employ it in her description of spiritual combat.

Both sides of her family had origins in nobility. Her father, Don Alonso de Cepeda, was the son of a Jewish merchant. Though he had converted to Christianity, Teresa's father was stigmatized for life by his Christian brethren. He was a holy man and, it appears, had little interest in getting ahead. Teresa's mother, Doña Beatriz de Ahumada, was Don Alonso's second wife. She was intelligent, beautiful, and wealthy, but giving birth to twelve children—three girls and nine boys—and bearing the responsibilities of marriage and family shortened her life; she died at thirty-three. Teresa was thirteen at the time.

From her autobiography, we can see that Teresa was an imaginative and intelligent child. Though she was the middle child in a large family, she held her ground with a vivacious personality, and her strong will enabled her to control her brothers. She was also quite pious, influenced by the example of her parents who, in her autobiography, she refers to as exemplars of virtue. Her father introduced her to good books, and her mother, to prayer and devotion to Mary.

According to a well-known story, when Teresa was six, she convinced her brother Rodrigo, who was four years older than her, to accompany her on an expedition to seek martyrdom from the Moors. Both children, only a mile out of town, were retrieved by an uncle who, by chance, passed them on the road. Teresa blamed the entire adventure on her brother, though she was the one who was in charge.

Later she also played at being a hermit with her brothers, persuading them to build hermitages in the garden. These adventures and imaginings may seem out of the ordinary, but, in fact, they were influenced not only by the pious example of her parents but also by the atmosphere òf Ávila. It was a town where cloisters and church activities were integral to the environment. Faith was the air that everyone breathed.

Entering Adolescence

When her mother died in 1528, Teresa mourned the loss and then turned her attention away from the pieties of her youth and toward the lure of worldly pleasures. She realized that she was attractive and became caught up in the desire to look pretty. "I began to dress in finery and to desire to please and look pretty, taking great care of my hands and hair and about perfumes and all the empty things in which one can indulge, and which were many, for I was very vain" (BL 2.2).

She and her mother had read novels of chivalry together, and her curiosity drove her to explore what it meant to be loved passionately like the ladies in these chivalric tales. Her father looked on, worried and disapproving.

Teresa's female cousin joined her in her flirtation with romance; both shared local gossip, flirtations, and love letters hidden from her father. All of this diversion drained her spirit and threatened her morality. She admits that it was her desire to preserve her honor that saved her and prevented loss of virtue. "I was extreme in my vain desire for my reputation, but the means necessary to preserve it I didn't take" (BL 2.4). As a spiritually mature woman in her late forties writing her autobiography, Teresa looked back at this time in her life with a disapproving and even harsh eye.

Teresa tried to keep her activity secret, but her father, Don Alonso, saw through the charade and sent his sixteen-year-old daughter to an Augustinian convent school, Our Lady of Grace. At first she was unhappy, but she settled in and found that "I was much more content than when in my father's house" (BL 2.8). She began to study prayer but found that her heart had hardened to the extent that "I could read the entire Passion without shedding a tear" (3.1).

Although Teresa had a sympathy for religious life, she had no desire to be a nun. At the same time, however, she feared marriage. She repented of the vanities of her youth, but her heart was still disoriented, caught between a call to religious life and a return to her worldly lifestyle.

Due to an inexplicable illness, which included high fevers and fainting, she was forced to leave the school and spend time convalescing, first at the home of her uncle and later with her older sister in a nearby hamlet. This would be the first of many illnesses during her very active life and would lead her to believe that from the beginning, her body had betrayed her. However, the illness gave her time to read and reflect. Following the example of her hermit-like uncle, she concentrated on the Fathers of the Church. It was while reading the *Letters of St. Jerome* that she found the courage to tell her father about the decision she had made: she wanted to enter the convent and become a nun. Her father refused, so Teresa left the house secretly and entered the Carmelite Monastery of the Incarnation.

The Carmelites

The Carmelites originated in the late twelfth century when a group of hermits settled on Mount Carmel, northeast of Galilee. These hermits were poor men seeking to follow Jesus Christ. Their story focused on two symbols: Mary, the Mother of God, and Elijah the prophet, who had found a home on Mount Carmel. Both figures embodied the vision of the early Carmelites and made clear the path to intimacy with God.

Sometime between 1206 and 1214, Albert of Jerusalem gave the hermits of Carmel a "way of life," a written rule for them that was later called the "primitive rule." Teresa found inspiration and guidance in the contemplative ideal encapsulated in this rule. She wrote:

So I say now that all of us who wear this holy habit of Carmel are called to prayer and contemplation. This call explains our origin; we are descendants of men who felt this call, of those holy fathers on Mount Carmel who in such great solitude and contempt for the world sought this treasure, this precious pearl of contemplation. . . . Yet few of us dispose ourselves that the Lord may communicate it to us. (IC V.1.2)

This rule was adapted through the centuries, and in Teresa's time, it was called the "mitigated rule." Women were given permission to enter the order in 1452, and soon the Carmelites spread through France, Italy, and Spain.

Does this vision of Carmel meet the needs of a postmodern world? According to Carmelite author Wilfrid McGreal, "The Carmelite tradition today would say . . . that listening, recognizing the wisdom of the heart, brings us to that contemplative state that opens us to God's loving presence. . . . This contemplative prayer . . . then draws us into solidarity with all who are in need of God's mercy."[6] Teresa herself emphasized that it is our love for others that is the key to determining the purity of our love for God.

The Monastery of the Incarnation

With her decision to enter the Monastery of the Incarnation, Teresa's dilemma was seemingly resolved. Though she had been previously unclear about the direction of her life, now she felt sure of her path and was committed to serving God. However, her desire to enter did not originate in the joyful spirit of one who is answering a call but rather evolved from the strong will of a young woman who feared hell and sought refuge behind convent walls.

The Monastery of the Incarnation housed about 180 nuns, and followed the mitigated rule, which meant that the discipline of the original primitive rule was relaxed. The nuns followed a regimen of hours in prayer, regular confession, and fasting, but they also had surprising freedom in what they could wear and how long they could be absent from the monastery. They could entertain friends and family in the parlor, and those with a substantial dowry could keep servants and live in separate suites. Because the house had no benefactor and the numbers were great, the nuns were encouraged to leave the convent to eat with family or friends.

Though the conditions were not ideal, Teresa found that she was happy in her new state of life and did not long to return home. This joy surprised her and began to soften her heart. "He gave me such great happiness at being in the religious state of life that it never left me up to this day, and God changed the dryness my soul experienced into the greatest tenderness" (BL 4.2). She found inspiration in the lives of some of the nuns but regretted that the hours in chapel were not complemented by meditation and contemplative prayer.

Illness

Teresa suffered poor health during her time in the monastery, and her symptoms became increasingly more serious; sometimes she would faint and nearly lose consciousness. Though her condition remained a mystery, it was generally attributed to heart problems. Her father arranged for the best doctors but to no avail. In desperation they turned to a female healer, and set out to meet her and arrange for treatment.

Along the way, they stayed with Don Alonso's brother, Don Pedro, who had already influenced Teresa's spiritual path by introducing her to the Church Fathers. This time Don Pedro suggested that Teresa read a book called *The Third Spiritual Alphabet* by Francisco de Osuna, which advocated recollection, an active focusing of inner attention, and total abandonment to God.

Teresa was delighted because her prayers were limited to vocal prayers and she was unsure about the practice of prayer in general. She invested herself fully in Osuna's book and marked her favorite passages as she read. No doubt she was captivated in the first chapter by the author's assurance that "friendship with God in this life is possible and not so very difficult and that love between the soul and God is even more intimate than between the highest ranking angels."[7] Further on, Osuna discusses the different kinds of silence, perhaps awakening and reinforcing the contemplative yearning in the depths of Teresa's heart.

Teresa's own practice at the time depended on using a book as a catalyst for prayer and as a way of stilling her rambling mind. Her fundamental way of prayer was to "keep Jesus Christ . . . present within me" (BL 4.7).

The "cure" for her illness failed and even made her worse, leaving her unable to move. She suffered greatly; the pain in her heart increased, and she grew thin and weak. "I remained in this excruciating state no more than three months, for it seemed impossible to be able to suffer so many ills together" (BL 5.8). Eventually, she became unconscious; a grave was dug, and her body was prepared for burial. She awoke to find wax on her eyelids.

Even when she returned to the convent, the paralysis continued, lingering for three years. When it abated, she was able to get around on her hands and knees. Accustomed to spending time in the infirmary, she longed for solitude so that she could pray. She was only twenty-five.

Conversion

Teresa found that her life at the Monastery of the Incarnation was superficial, a sociable atmosphere lacking any inner depth. Though aware of the risks of spending time in the parlor with friends and relatives, receiving gifts and charming visitors with her wit and sense of humor, she continued to socialize, and her guilt deepened.

Even though she had once taken to heart the words of Osuna's *The Third Spiritual Alphabet,* her prayer had not progressed beyond oral repetition. She found time for solitude and enjoyed talking about God, but she did not experience the presence of the divine. At one point she gave up prayer completely. However, after the death of her father in 1543, she reached out to a confessor. He advised her not to let go of prayer because it would never cease to profit her soul. As a result, she began praying again. From that moment, she never faltered, even though prayer itself was responsible for intensifying her awareness of living a contradiction.

For twenty years of convent life, Teresa's calm and cheerful outward appearance belied her inner torment. The more she became aware of divine goodness, the more she recognized the full force of her harmful attachment to the world. Around the age of forty, Teresa came to the turning point, a conversion experience. Her exhaustion from her long struggle—both physical and spiritual—made her vulnerable to the grace she would receive as she gazed at a starkly realistic image of Christ in agony being scourged at the pillar. She was totally overcome with grief. "Beholding it I was utterly distressed in seeing Him that way, for it well represented what He suffered for us. I felt so keenly aware of how poorly I thanked Him for those wounds that . . . my heart broke" (BL 9.1). From this point on, she placed her complete trust in God and no longer questioned the direction of her life: Christ was at the center.

She read St. Augustine's *Confessions* and identified with his account of hearing a voice in the garden speaking to his heart, calling him to conversion. Her prayer life changed: she was now certain that she loved God and that God loved her, and her prayer became more aligned with her temperament. She claimed that she had difficulty using her imagination or reason as an aid to recollection but found ways to use both. She favored a meditation with simple reflection in which she could identify with Christ's feelings, particularly at those times when he was alone and suffering, like in the Garden of Gethsemane.

Teresa also discovered that reading books and gazing at nature helped her to focus her attention on the presence of Christ within her. In time she felt this presence with certainty: "It used to happen, when I represented Christ within me in order to place myself in His presence, or even while reading, that a feeling of the presence of God would come upon me unexpectedly so that I could in no way doubt He was within me or I totally immersed in Him" (BL 10.1).

The Reform

As Teresa's prayer life matured, sometimes accompanied by extraordinary experiences, she was often criticized or doubted, particularly by confessors who were baffled by the young woman. However, one man in particular, the Franciscan Peter of Alcantara, who was held in the highest esteem as a spiritual director, defended her against her critics. He was also a reformer of his order, refocusing the friars on their life of poverty and austerity. Teresa had the greatest love and respect for him and would soon follow in his footsteps, spearheading change in her own Carmelite community. For his part, Peter gave her his complete support and was able to pass along practical knowledge necessary for the formation of new reform convents.

By 1560 Teresa had become interested in establishing Carmelite houses in which the primitive rule could be lived. She felt called to a simpler, more contemplative lifestyle that emulated the early monks. For Teresa, the community at the Incarnation was too large and not conducive to true friendship with her sisters and intimacy with God. There was also so much contact with the outside world that distractions became overwhelming. Yet doubts about the future haunted her: "There were doubts as to whether those who lived here would be happy with so much austerity. . . . All that the Lord had commanded me, and the great deal of advice, and the prayers . . . , all was erased from my memory as though it had never been" (BL 36.7).

Nevertheless, Teresa took things into her own hands and, at forty-five years of age, not only admitted that she needed greater discipline and sacrifice, but forged ahead in spite of her dread of what the future might hold.

Not only did Teresa have a difficult time with her fellow nuns at the Incarnation, but she was denounced from the pulpits of Ávila (how could she, a woman, presume to follow in the footsteps of the Desert Fathers and other saintly ascetics?) and lost the support of her Carmelite provincial. Teresa was prepared to give up the project, and for five or six months took no action, but one day "the Lord told me not to be anxious, that that affliction would soon end"(BL 33.8). Soon she found herself in harmony with new leadership and was free to continue her work.

St. Joseph's Monastery

The house that was to become St. Joseph's Monastery was bought in secret to avoid angering both those in the city who objected to funding yet another monastery and a number of the Sisters of the Incarnation, who continued to disapprove. Teresa's own dream was reinforced by experiences such as a vision she had of St. Clare of Assisi, a reformer in her own right, who "appeared to me with striking beauty. She told me to take courage and to continue on with what I had begun, that she would help me" (BL 33.13).

In 1562 Teresa and several sisters, including novices, opened St. Joseph's. Friends and supporters filled the small chapel. The community became known as Discalced (barefoot) Carmelites, a name that expressed their devotion to poverty.

Only two days after the opening of the new convent, the city council called a meeting that included representatives from all the religious orders, and it was decided that the new Convent of St. Joseph must be closed. A Dominican friend was the only one to defend Teresa's vision, and even he disagreed with her vow of poverty. Teresa was confined to her cell at the Incarnation while the debate raged. The prioress ordered her to have nothing to do with the matter. Two years passed before there was a compromise and the foundation was allowed to continue. Teresa was given permission to leave the Incarnation and live at St. Joseph's.

Though troubled by the future of the nuns that she had convinced to follow her to St. Joseph's, Teresa was unmoved by all the defamatory things said about her, buoyed by her confidence that she had not offended her order or God. Teresa referred to her five years living at St. Joseph's, beginning in 1563, as the happiest and most restful of her life. She was finally able to live the life that she had yearned for and fought so hard to establish. Happiness is contagious, and the number of sisters who joined her grew quickly.

The group was small, so the atmosphere in the humble dwelling of mud and stone was intimate, like a family. Since their life was monastic and influenced by the spirit of the hermits, much of the day was spent in solitude. Teresa herself modeled this ascetic disposition through her austerity, mortification, solitude, and prayer. Though Teresa's own mortification would be considered extreme and something we could not relate to today, she never advocated excessive penances for others. The nuns prayed, read, and worked in the quiet of their cells. Prayer was given the highest priority, and the *Constitutions,* or rule, that Teresa drew up included the time and manner in which the Daily Office was to be observed, the days that Communion was to be received, and the spiritual books that should be read.

They fasted for long periods, embraced the spirit of poverty, and earned what they could through sewing and spinning, though it was a small amount, barely enough for survival. The atmosphere of the community, however, was not heavy and serious but light and joyful. Teresa had little patience with dour-faced saints who made virtue seem distasteful and difficult. There may have been seriousness and silence in the strict enclosure, but this was interspersed with times of joy and laughter, with feast days being the occasion for music, dance, and singing.

After a few months of enjoying the freedom of being an ordinary nun, with some reluctance Teresa obeyed the wishes of the bishop and became the prioress. She held that, unlike the common social practice in sixteenth-century Spain, there would be no distinction between the sisters because of honor or rank. All titles and family distinctions were left behind. She was well aware of the harm done in the name of family loyalty. Teresa wanted separation from the world and from social posturing that had influenced the nuns at the Monastery of the Incarnation. She knew that cutting ties with family members would be a difficult form of detachment, particularly in a society that prized honor and cultivated inordinate attachment to family, but she insisted that such a choice was necessary for a full dedication to the service of God. Everyone was equal; everyone shared in household duties. She was said to comment that "God walks also among pots and pans."[8]

She invited St. John of the Cross, who had helped her found other monasteries, to be a chaplain at the Monastery of the Incarnation. John had also established a home for the first reformed Carmelite friars in Duruelo, a tiny house that was more like a hovel thirty miles outside Ávila. The house may have been poor, but it symbolized the desire of both Teresa and John to embrace poverty as a door that opened into divine love. John, a mystic and a poet, played a major part in Teresa's personal life as confessor, "the father of my soul," and friend, though their personalities were very different. At one point, John, holding out against strong opposition to the reform, was imprisoned for nine months by a non-reformed provincial. He later escaped and continued his work for the reform.

Continued Reform

The fertile ground provided by the way of life at St. Joseph's became the seedbed for Teresa's creative energy. In the first years at St. Joseph's, Teresa had written not one but two versions of her *Life* at the request of her confessor. Since the nuns at St. Joseph's did not have access to it, they pleaded with her to write something for them. Teresa responded with *The Way of Perfection*, which addressed specifically the way of life that should be practiced at St. Joseph's, although in her informal style it goes off-track to include other subjects. *The Way of Perfection* offers us a clear picture of Teresa's way of life as outlined in her *Constitutions*. It includes topics such as detachment, love, and, of course, humility, since humility, in particular, forms the basis for prayer.

Due to a surprise visit by the superior general of the Carmelites in the spring of 1567—no Carmelite general had visited the communities in Spain—Teresa found herself on the defensive. Since most Carmelites had disapproved of her reform community, and the superior general had not given her permission to establish St. Joseph's (she did have the approval of her provincial superior and the bishop), she feared that the superior general would order her and her sisters to return to the Incarnation Monastery.

In fact, the superior general, after hearing Teresa's story and the founding of the convent, was moved to tears and gave her permission to establish more foundations, even promising to censure anyone who hindered her. After more than four years in a quiet life of prayer, her imagination came alive with the possibility of establishing more centers of prayer. She could have remained a mystic and influenced others behind the walls of her convent with her writings and prayer, but she found that her contemplation was driving her toward action. She had thought that she was only a poor Discalced nun without material resources, but she had the personal attributes of common sense and practicality—not to mention courage and hope—that would help her on the road ahead.

Teresa would be on the road for the rest of her life, traveling throughout Spain, opening the doors of new foundations, and monitoring those that had been established. She was a fifty-two-year-old woman who was never in good health and who had spent most of her life in the comfort of a home or the seclusion of a convent. Now she had to bear the travails of traveling in covered wagons with solid wooden wheels, rumbling along through snow and rain, intense heat, and bitter cold. The nuns consoled themselves with the beautiful scenery or with rest stops beside a stream or in the woods.

The wagons themselves became traveling convents because the nuns made every attempt to preserve a sense of enclosure, with a schedule for prayer and silence and intermittent conversations about God. They always wore their veils and preserved their privacy. Though threatened by danger and traveling without any comforts, they found strength in their small community.

Teresa herself, convinced that she was carrying out God's plan, seems to have adapted and even thrived on the balance between a contemplative and active life. Despite her physical impediments, she continued to establish new foundations, often encountering resistance. In fact, between the years 1576 and 1579, the struggles between the Discalced Reform and the Calced Carmelites escalated. During this time, Teresa felt that all her life's work was in jeopardy. However, in the midst of this turmoil, she found even greater determination to continue her work, and even wrote her masterpiece, *The Interior Castle*.

"How Very Long Is the Road of This Life"

Teresa admitted that in her youth, the thought of death haunted and terrified her. Later, as a mature nun, she longed for death because of her desire for complete union with God. At the same time, she recognized that she was being called to embrace life fully while on earth. However, at the age of sixty-five, she had acquired a fundamental detachment, in which neither life nor death concerned her.

In 1582, after a year of difficult travel and ill health, the nuns arrived at the Alba convent doors. Teresa was so weak that she could not speak and could no longer conceal her pain and exhaustion. She longed to return home, but on September 29 she went to bed and would never leave it. A severe hemorrhage depleted the little strength she had. In her last days on earth, Teresa was surrounded by loving nuns and was attended by Ana de San Bartolomé, a nurse and a companion for many years.

On October 3, she received the Sacrament of Extreme Unction and made her last confession. During the night, she was heard to repeat a penitential psalm over and over again: "A broken and a contrite heart, Lord, thou wilt not despise. . . . / Cast me not away from thy face."[9] Even at the end, the memory of her sins tormented her. On October 4, the feast of Saint Francis of Assisi, Teresa died in the arms of her faithful Ana.

> How very long
> is the road of this life,
> a painful dwelling,
> a hard exile.
> Oh, adored Master,
> take me from here!
> *Anxious to see You,*
> *I want to die.* (P 21)

Overview

The chapters that follow introduce Teresa's map for the journey of prayer as outlined in *The Interior Castle*. Though this is my primary source, I will draw on other writings by Teresa, particularly *The Way of Perfection* and her autobiography, *The Book of Her Life*. Both of these latter works are an important prelude to *The Interior Castle*, and reading them—which I strongly suggest—provides a rich context for Teresa's spiritual vision.

The first two chapters invite you to the prayer journey by focusing on two fundamental themes for Teresa: the turn inward and the virtues of charity, detachment, and humility, which she considered essential for growth in prayer.

Chapters 3–5 describe the life of prayer as it unfolds in the dwellings of the interior castle, and the final chapter summarizes the prayer journey using the metaphor of a contemplative walk.

You are invited to move with Teresa into the deeper dimensions of life and love and discover your own path of prayer with her counsel. The questions at the end of each chapter are meant to offer avenues for reflection.

My hope is that you will discover, as I did, that even given her own unique and challenging life circumstances and the great differences between our culture and hers, Teresa speaks to us today. She redirects our attention in the midst of our sometimes chaotic lives to what is most important—namely, the presence of Christ—and invites us to open our hearts and listen. If you want to "see" God for yourself and uncover your own "interior castle"—your path of prayer—then, says Teresa, let me be your guide.

CHAPTER ONE

Turning Inward

Turn your eyes inward and look within yourself.
—The Way of Perfection, 29.2

A good friend introduced me to the painting *Footprints in the Desert* by the British artist Albert Herbert, which represents a common approach to the spiritual journey. At the bottom of the painting is a trail of footprints through a stream and into a long stretch of desert. The desert ends at a mountain range, and at the top of one of the mountains a girl dances, expressing the freedom and joy of one who has reached the culmination of a difficult spiritual quest. In this painting by Herbert, God is "out there," separate from us, waiting for our arrival, and we have to travel a difficult and demanding path to reach our goal.

Traditionally, the prayer journey involves a movement outward, across deserts, up mountains or ladders, in order to seek God who is beyond us. In contrast, Teresa invites us inward, because we already possess all that we need. God is present at the center of our being, so there is no reason to search elsewhere. We are already at home but do not realize it. Our task, then, is to wake up to Christ calling us home. The treasure within us awaits our attention.

And if, by chance, you do not know
where you will find Me,
do not wander to and fro,

for if you want to find Me,
you must find Me in you. (P 29)

Our Soul Is Like a Castle

Consider our soul to be like a castle made entirely out of a
diamond or of very clear crystal. (The Interior Castle, I.1.1)

Teresa's primary image for the journey—the metaphor of the
castle in her classic work *The Interior Castle*—came to her
in a vision. It may have been reinforced in her unconscious
by a number of influences: the walled town of Castile where
she lived and the battlefields close by, where in her lifetime
Christians fought against the Moors; the tales of chivalry she
read as a young girl; and Francis de Osuna's *The Third Spiritual Alphabet,* a book that influenced Teresa's prayer and that
uses war metaphors freely to describe the necessity of guard-
ing the heart against the onslaught of invaders.

Inspired by the beautiful and romantic setting of a castle, Teresa
imagined that it would be a provocative image for the soul. She
knew quite well that the story of the soul's journey would evade
any attempt to describe her experience of it. But with the instincts
of a poet, she spontaneously drew on images and metaphors that
she trusted to express the mysteries she wanted to explore, like
love, faith, and, in particular, the human soul. Her creative imagination, grounded in intuition, feeling, and dreaming, revealed
itself more in symbols and images than in conceptual ideas. Her
theology, then, is not inclined toward the development of ideas
and concepts but begins with experience and then communicates
its message through symbols and images.

Teresa uses this image of the castle to remind us of our own inherent beauty as people created in the image and likeness of God and possessing the capacity for intimacy with the divine. For Teresa, the soul was not a sterile abstraction but was dynamic and fertile—perhaps like a womb—and capable of a continuous process of birthing. The soul expands with grace, and the different dwelling places have an organic quality, rising up like petals of a rose from a shared center. Teresa finds it difficult to contain herself: "I don't find anything comparable to the magnificent beauty of a soul and its marvelous capacity. Indeed, our intellects, however keen, can hardly comprehend it, just as they cannot comprehend God" (IC I.1.1).

At the center, God, the King of the castle, awaits to embrace us. The center of our soul, says Teresa, "is the main dwelling place where the very secret exchanges between God and the soul take place" (IC I.1.3). God continually invites the person to find a home in which to dwell in truth and love. Our journey, then, is primarily focused on one thing alone: union with God.

Using this metaphor of the castle, Teresa invites us on a pilgrimage into the depths of our being. As we move inward, our lives begin to gravitate around this center, and the result is a sense of wholeness and inner peace.

Instead of the confusion and chaos outside the wall controlling our destiny—which many experience as a normal way of life—Teresa wants us to turn inward and explore. "There is a great difference in the ways one may be inside the castle. For there are many souls who are in the outer courtyard . . . and don't care at all about entering the castle, nor do they know what lies within that most precious place, nor who is within, nor even how many rooms it has. You have already heard in some books on prayer that the soul is advised to enter within itself; well that's the very thing I'm advising" (IC I.1.5).

WITHIN ONESELF IS THE BEST PLACE TO LOOK

Within oneself, very clearly, is the best place to look;
and it's not necessary to go to heaven, nor any further than
our own selves; for to do so is to tire the spirit and distract
the soul, without gaining as much fruit.
(The Book of Her Life, 40.6)

Teresa's insistence that we look within echoes the concern of St. Augustine, who wrote, "You were within me, while I was outside. . . . You were with me, but I was not with you."[10] For both, it is a simple question: why bother with any other path, no matter how extraordinary, when the inward journey will take us home? Why seek God in a multitude of places when you can find God in your own heart?

The spiritual journey, for Teresa, is a process of centering, moving ever deeper from the circumference of our life to its depths, from the externals to the mysterious inner realm where Christ waits. She calls us to risk this journey into the unknown based on our trust that our longing for God will guide us and give us strength.

Today there is a danger of misunderstanding her metaphor of inwardness. Many assume that to move inward involves a process of introspection, or perhaps self-exploration through psychological analysis. These approaches may be helpful tools, but they are primarily self-oriented. For both Teresa and Augustine, the point is not to focus on the self but to uncover the presence of divine love within oneself. We do not have to bring God into our lives; we have to realize that we already possess divine love.

For Teresa, it is a matter of listening to the deepest call that draws us within ourselves and then allowing that call to reorient our lives around the one thing that is most important, our ultimate concern. It is a journey into love that awaits us. "Anyone who loves me will keep my word, and my Father will love him, and we shall come to him and make a home in him" (John 14:23). We allow this love to lead us home to the source of our lives. We need not do anything extraordinary, Teresa assures us; we only need to remain humbly attentive to the call. We should not be looking for visions and unusual experiences but only for solitude so that we can be present to the One who is already present to us.

KNOWING OURSELVES IS SO IMPORTANT

Knowing ourselves is something so important that I wouldn't want any relaxation ever in this regard, however high you may have climbed. (The Interior Castle, I.2.9)

Thomas Merton once asked, "What can we gain by sailing to the moon if we are not able to cross the abyss that separates us from ourselves?"[11] Teresa was well aware of this abyss. She stressed that it exists because of a lack of self-knowledge. In other words, we are so taken with a life based on appearances that we do not have a relationship with our own center; we do not know who we truly are.

We may be created in the image of God, but we live as if we are strangers, unable to enter the house in which we were born. No wonder Teresa proposes growth in self-knowledge as the "safe and level path" (IC I.2.9). This leads us through the rooms of the castle, not in a programmed fashion, advancing from one stage to another, but rather in a more creative way. We may pass from exterior to interior, with doors opening in revelation and closing in hiddenness. We may even uncover secrets in unlikely places.

Without the knowledge of our life in God, we assume that we must create our own reality. As a result, we perpetuate an illusion that keeps us isolated and unhappy—namely, that we are separate from God. Teresa insisted that self-knowledge is so important that no matter where we are on the spiritual journey, beginner or advanced, we must cultivate it. "You mustn't think of these dwelling places in such a way that each one would follow in file after the other; but turn your eyes toward the center, which is the room or royal chamber where the King stays" (IC 1.2.8). We only know who we truly are, says Teresa, when we have our sights on God alone.

For Teresa, the journey toward greater self-knowledge is at the same time a journey toward God. With greater self-awareness, we discover the tremendous mystery and power of God and our true condition as dependent creatures with our own beauty and dignity. Throughout her writings Teresa repeatedly insisted—perhaps in a harsher tone than our modern ear would prefer—that she herself was completely reliant on God's mercy and love.

THOSE IN THE OUTER COURTYARD

For there are many souls who are in the outer courtyard . . .
and don't care at all about entering the castle, nor do they

know what lies within that most precious place, nor who is
within, nor even how many rooms it has.
(The Interior Castle, I.1.5)

Take the example of Fred, who has come to a point in his life where the usual pleasures are no longer enough. Rather than pursuing such outward activities as playing golf, traveling, and immersing himself in work, he finds himself turning inward, reflecting and listening to a faint but persistent whisper. At one time in his life, he ignored this inner voice, but now it seems more real and urgent than ever before. He once had a great interest in the mystics and now begins again to read all that he can find by Thomas Merton and Henri Nouwen, as well as John of the Cross and St. Teresa. Reading these spiritual works assures him that he needs to trust this mysterious call and allow it to guide him. He realizes that his many activities have evolved into a blanket of noise and confusion, muffling any attempt at deep listening and forcing him to live on the periphery of his life. It is now clear to him: he must learn to listen.

Teresa addresses those who are dissatisfied, weary of chasing dreams on the surface of life, or hungering for something more substantial. They want to experience God, not as a distant figure, but as a consistent presence of divine love, a friend who is near and available. They are open to letting the Spirit draw them beyond thinking about God and into the experience of God's presence.

Mesmerized by externals, we can easily forget the reality of the inner depths; the possibility of hearing a call addressed to us can be drowned out by all that is going on around us. We are handicapped by being busy, tired, and not having enough time. The parade of life events does not abate but demands our attention more and more. Eventually, we are transfixed by the outer sphere of our lives. Even when we hear stories of a hidden depth, we do not quite believe them, or we assume that it is a realm for others to explore. And so Teresa pleads with us: leave behind the confusion and chaos outside the walls that have wearied your soul for so long and enter into the castle.

Nevertheless, it is difficult to trust this inner journey; the depth seems imposing, particularly to those who have not explored it. There is a tale about a frog who lives in a pool with other frogs. One day this frog goes searching for adventure and stumbles upon a large body of water—the ocean. She stands in awe gazing at the endless horizon, unable to comprehend the vastness. Then, eager to share her adventure, she returns to the pond and reports her astounding experience to the rest of the frogs. Hearing her tale, they turn away in disbelief. How could such an immense body of water really exist? And why would they want to explore elsewhere when they already possess everything they need in the security and comfort of their pond?

We Must Disengage Ourselves

We must, then, disengage ourselves from everything
so as to approach God interiorly and even in the midst of
occupations withdraw within ourselves.
(The Way of Perfection, 29.5)

Do we believe in our own path of self-knowledge? Do we trust, as Teresa did, that even under layers of darkness, the divine inner light will prevail and lead the way?

Teresa would insist that no matter where we are in our lives right now or how great a sinner we think we are, in the end grace is stronger than sin. However, we may find her words difficult to trust because they are contrary to our tendency to idolize individual accomplishments. We assume too quickly that the sweat and toil of our hard work is more efficient than grace.

If we are willing to answer the call to transformation, Teresa insists, we need to be open to the light of Christ within us and allow that light to lead us. She is primarily concerned with the life of freedom that results when compulsions and the pull of desires lessen, when the ego becomes porous and we are able to be guided in love by the Holy Spirit. "It should be kept in mind here," she writes, "that the fount, the shining sun that is in the center of the soul, does not lose its beauty and splendor; it is always present" (IC I.2.3). However, she warns, this love is present only if we choose to depend on it and find our home in it.

It is important to realize that although Teresa was a cloistered contemplative, she does not suggest that we remove ourselves from our social environment in order to have a relationship with God. She invites us to preserve our solitude in the midst of our everyday routine, to respond when we feel the nudge inward and acknowledge the nearness of divine presence by stepping aside. Even if we hear nothing, God is speaking. "What we ourselves can do is to strive to be alone. . . . Do you think He is silent? Even though we do not hear Him, He speaks well to the heart when we beseech Him from the heart" (WP 24.5)

By taking this moment to be aware of God's presence, we realize that we are not the originators of our actions or our prayer but that we depend on the Spirit of love to guide and inform all that we are and do. Teresa was not interested in avoiding the difficulties of daily life. Rather, she emphasized the need to use our trials as a path of transformation and, in particular, to embrace our suffering and the suffering of others so that we might grow in compassion.

THE GATE OF ENTRY IS PRAYER

The door of entry to this castle is prayer and reflection.
(The Interior Castle, I.7)

The journey inward away from the turmoil at the circumference of our lives, says Teresa, is only possible through prayer. She warns, "Don't let anyone deceive you by showing you a road other than that of prayer" (WP 21.6). Prayer is as essential as food, and without it we risk dying of hunger. For Teresa, a Christian life without prayer is impossible because through prayer we recover and nurture our true identity in God.

Prayer is not primarily about thinking or speaking or even about praying at particular times; rather, it is the posture of our hearts before God. Our entire lives are being addressed continually. The primary question is this one: is our heart leaning toward God, listening, or turned away from God, caught up in the turmoil?

Our hearts naturally gravitate toward God when they have the opportunity, just as seeds turn toward the light, but many do not recognize this truth. I asked a group of undergraduates whether they prayed. Most responded, "No." Then I asked if they found themselves talking to God at times during the day, when they were driving or had some down time, perhaps spontaneously asking for help or expressing gratitude. Several admitted turning their attention to God but said they did not think of it as prayer. In one case, a woman who said she struggled with prayer used the time alone after work each day, when she was walking her dog, to reflect on her life. She looked forward to these walks because, as she put it, they somehow cleansed her soul and renewed her spirit for the next day, and during these times she often shared her feelings with God. When I asked her if this could be her prayer, she hesitated and then a wave of recognition crossed her face.

For Teresa, prayer is opening our hearts to the presence of God within us, a spontaneous pouring out to Christ. It can take the form of a conversation, sharing with Jesus the fears and desires of the heart, but this is not conversation in the typical, casual sense. When we relate to God authentically, we become aware of our complete dependence on him as the source of our lives, so our prayer often expresses a humble giftedness, a thankfulness for our own being and for all that we have received.

Another deeper form of prayer goes beyond words toward greater and greater simplicity. We learn to wait in stillness and silence as God takes over our lives. We do not try to express our dependence on God but rather experience our dependence in a silence that enfolds and nurtures us. The heart rests in God and self-consciousness fades. We realize that separation from God is an illusion stitched together by a multitude of our thoughts and feelings. Union is the fundamental reality, not separation; we are in God.

This prayer without words has no goal. We are not trying to find God because we are already in God's presence, so we learn to wait with an open heart. It is important to realize that such simple prayer, which is grounded in silence, is not the same as contemplation but rather prepares us for contemplation. Contemplation, which Teresa introduces as the "prayer of quiet," is pure gift, a total awareness of God's presence, the highest degree of wordless prayer. "In this contemplation . . . we don't do anything ourselves. Neither do we labor, nor do we bargain, nor is anything else necessary—because everything else is an impediment and hindrance—than to say *fiat voluntas tua*: Your will, Lord, be done in me" (WP 32.10).

This Prayer, a Little Spark of Love

This prayer, then, is a little spark of the Lord's true love which He begins to enkindle in the soul; and He desires that the soul grow in the understanding of what this love accompanied by delight is.
(The Book of Her Life, 15.4)

If we think of God's presence not as a fire or an earthquake but as a gentle tug of love, the wafting of a gentle breeze (1 Kings 19:11-13) or a spark, then we have to wonder about when we were called. When did God first address us? Perhaps, looking back, we have an awareness of our entire history claimed by God from the beginning.

In her poem "The Thread," Denise Levertov describes "a thread / or net of threads / finer than cobweb" that has been tugging at our souls from the time we were in our mothers' womb.[12] She observes that this tug elicits feelings of wonder and awe, not fear. Later in her own life, Levertov recognized that this tug on her soul was a call to conversion and, at the same time, a validation of her vocation as a poet.

When we awaken to the call of love, we discover a spiritual energy that has charged our souls from the beginning. The question is, are we aware of the "thread," and do we reflect on it and cherish it?

Jesus invites us to walk with him, says Teresa, and recognize that we have always been loved. This love invites communication. Our desire to respond will eventually lead to an unbroken communion in which life itself becomes prayer. No longer can we accept that faith is limited to belief in dogma; it has come alive in the person of Jesus Christ: "For everyone who asks receives; everyone who searches finds; everyone who knocks will have the door opened" (Luke 11:10).

To embrace this journey fully, Teresa suggests that we see God as a friend, but, more than this, an intimate friend who knows us more than we know ourselves. This intimacy invites us beyond a sporadic involvement. We are to be in the presence of our friend and experience the joy and giftedness of this relationship continually.

So how do we prepare for the journey? Or for that matter, how do we get in touch with this thread of love? Here is a suggestion I have used on retreats. First, begin by giving yourself the opportunity for an emotionally honest look at your life and your relationship with God at the present moment. We reflect on many things but rarely on our inner life and our relationship with Christ. How would you describe your spiritual life today? Is there an image that comes to mind that symbolizes this relationship for you?

Second, trust that grace—the expression of divine love—has always been active in your life, like a thread tugging at you from the beginning, though you may not have been aware of it. List the times when God has broken through and touched your life. Continue to add to this list over time, and perhaps you will discover that grace has been the thread of your journey.

Remember not only the outstanding examples of being touched by divine love, but the more subtle ones, like the times when the spirit provided you with the strength, courage, or hope that you needed. For instance, maybe you reached out to someone and received no gratitude in return, or you forgave someone and were not rewarded with a restoration of the relationship. Have you ever made a decision based on an inner conviction in spite of opposition? Have you ever loved God, though you were no longer supported by feelings of divine presence?

Search your history and be alert to all such signs of grace; see how these take the form of your life story. Becoming more conscious of this thread of love is one of the most powerful ways to pray. Returning to this thread and recalling examples from it keep us from becoming lost when we no longer sense God's loving presence.

Turning to Look at God

In the measure you desire Him, you will find Him.
He so esteems our turning to look at Him.
(The Way of Perfection, 26.3)

We may assume that we turn to God first in prayer, but Teresa emphasizes that it is God who first gazed at us, who first loved us unconditionally and brought us into being. God continues to look at us lovingly, searching for room in our hearts throughout the day. Knowing this, how can we not turn our attention to God? "I'm not asking you to do anything more than look at Him. For who can keep you from turning the eyes of your soul toward this Lord, even if you do so just for a moment if you can't do more? . . . Your Spouse never takes His eyes off you" (WP 26.3). For Teresa, this gaze in which we keep our eyes on Christ, our constant companion, is our prayer.

It takes a lifetime, however, to accept this gaze of love and learn how to respond to it. How receptive are we to the loving gaze of someone close to us? How much more difficult to bear the look of unconditional love? Can we imagine that God sees something extraordinarily beautiful in us?

When the rich young man approached Jesus and offered to sacrifice everything for eternal life, Jesus responded with a tender gaze and "was filled with love for him" (Mark 10:21). This gaze invited the young man to a loving union with God, but it also called for transformation. Christ did not stand separate from the young man as judge or observer but called him from within himself, as One who knew him intimately and saw the total truth of who he was—all his strengths and weaknesses, his charades and giftedness. When the young man saw himself mirrored in this divine loving gaze, it startled him because suddenly he realized his true identity and the sacrifice necessary to uncover it. God's gaze radiates from the center of our being and invites a response. Will we pay attention or not? The starting point for our journey of inner transformation is the gift of this gaze and our willingness to respond to it. Teresa asks simply: why not return this loving gaze and look upon the One who always looks upon us?

Returning this gaze does not mean seeing Christ as an object separate from us but rather recognizing that we are already in

Christ and that the presence of Christ is in some way the very ground of our awareness. So to gaze at Christ is a gentle glance recognizing that Christ is alive within me. However, like the young man we hesitate and draw back in fear, not wanting to see the truth and wary of how unconditional love will change us. For those who encounter this gaze and remain vulnerable to it, everything changes: social conditioning and unhealthy attachments are released in favor of an inward adventure in pursuit of love.

At the end of her autobiography, Teresa describes her own encounter with God's gaze of love: "Once while I was reciting . . . the hours of the Divine Office, my soul suddenly became recollected; and it seemed to me to be like a brightly polished mirror, without any part on the back or sides or top or bottom that wasn't totally clear. In its center Christ, our Lord, was shown to me. . . . It seemed to me I saw Him clearly in every part of my soul, as though in a mirror" (BL 40.5).

This experience became a reminder to her of how easily darkness of sin can hide the soul from love, and it assured her that those who know this gaze of love will remember that God is not outside somewhere, but is instead waiting for them within their very selves.

Often we become aware of this gaze in surprising ways, and the experience leaves us in wonder and awe. It may occur, for example, through an encounter with a child or in the presence of the Eucharist. Dr. Ewert Cousins, a respected scholar and a humble and gracious man whom I came to know through a summer-long seminar on mysticism, reveals this turning point in his life. He writes:

That Sunday I was kneeling in chapel for the Benediction service and something happened. I was teaching Catechism to little kids on the Indian reservation and a little girl came up and hugged me. It was the first feeling of affection I felt in myself in months. Then that afternoon in chapel I was kneeling and looking at the monstrance exposed holding the Eucharistic bread. And I had a tremendous, overwhelming experience that I could love God. I just never had anything like that in my life. And it came up *in my body, pouring out into consciousness*. . . . My whole life is contained in this one experience from here on out.[13]

This experience demonstrates how God's gaze can be transformative for those who are open to it. It can change us forever, filling us with grace, calming our anxieties, and bringing hope to those dark parts of our lives by banishing fear, hatred, jealousy, and distrust.

If we ever doubt our path—and it can be profoundly challenging at times—we turn to face God and see the look in his eyes. We may not be very good lovers now, but as Teresa assures us, God will continue to transform us more and more. We have no need to protect ourselves and nothing to fear. So we must release our anxiety, for our path is forever being renewed and made whole through the mutual gaze of love between ourselves and God: "Of you my heart has said, 'Seek his face!'" (Psalm 27:8).

DRAW NEAR

Draw near, then, to this good Master with strong determination to learn what He teaches you. (The Way of Perfection, 26.10)

Teresa urges us to draw near to Christ in prayer so that our souls can be fed. We are always in Christ's presence—Christ is always looking at us—but we need to cultivate an openness through our practice. "Though we are always in the presence of God, it seems to me the manner is different with those who practice prayer, for they are aware that He is looking at them. With others, it can happen that several days pass without their recalling that God sees them" (BL 8.2).

Initially, our experience of intimacy with Christ may be intermittent, but eventually it becomes more continuous, more integrated into our lives as our prayer becomes more interior. We begin, however, by setting aside time to converse with Christ as with a friend, talking with Christ throughout the day about our difficulties, anxieties, joys, and hopes. Our intention is not to think about Jesus but to enter into a truly personal relationship with Him; to cultivate a simple loving attentiveness that we would find in a close friendship. "Mental prayer in my opinion," says Teresa, "is nothing else than an intimate sharing between friends; it means taking time frequently to be alone with Him who we know loves us" (BL 8.5).

In the classic fable *The Little Prince,* the fox gives us some insight into what a personal, passionate relationship might entail. The fox establishes a friendship with the prince by suggesting a ritual of meeting at a certain time each day. The encounter brings anticipation at first, but then grows into a commitment as they sit a little closer each day. The fox insists that this ritual is essential if friends are to understand and learn to love one another and that it will involve patience and heartfelt attention.[14]

Teresa encourages us to develop the habit of being alone with Christ at regular times each day—counsel that we may have heard many times but nevertheless have found difficult to incorporate into our busy lives. This habit of prayer, she says, becomes the axis around which the rest of life turns; it prevents us from detouring into worry and anxiety, no matter how potent their effect on us. Through prayer, we reinforce our awareness that Christ loves us, and this trust becomes integrated in all parts of our lives and centers our attention. She instructed her sisters to pray with confidence and love and to develop a core from which they could love both God and neighbor.

She adds, however, that it is not the amount of time we spend in prayer that is critical but the way in which our prayer is expressed in our actions: "It is not the length of time spent in prayer that benefits one; when the time is spent as well in good works, it is a help in preparing the soul for the enkindling of love. The soul may thereby be better prepared in a very short time than through many hours of reflection" (F 5.17).

Keeping Our Eyes Fixed

O Lord, how true that all harm comes to us from not keeping our eyes fixed on You. . . . We meet with a thousand falls and obstacles and lose the way because we don't keep our eyes . . . on the true way. (The Way of Perfection, 16.11)

The mindfulness of Christ's presence nurtured in times of prayer flows out into daily life, strengthening our desire to live more consciously in the presence of Jesus in every aspect of our lives. In other words, we grow in our trust that he walks at our side and supports us whether we are in times of quiet or crisis.

For Teresa, to pray unceasingly does not involve applying a conventional form of prayer to our daily lives but of attuning ourselves to our heart's deepest desire and allowing it to surface into consciousness throughout the day. Teresa asks only that we turn away from our preoccupations for a moment and give our attention to Christ and glance in his direction. Eventually, our gaze will become more consistent and our listening to the divine will be more sensitive, even in the midst of daily concerns.

This sense of Christ's abiding presence while walking through life's passages is truly a gift, one that leads us through the doorway of death. The priest and author Anthony de Mello tells the story of a priest who visits a dying man in his home. When the priest asks the man about an empty chair near the bed, he replies that he imagines that Jesus is sitting in the chair, so he talks with Jesus as he would talk to a friend. Later, after the man dies, his daughter tells the priest that when she found her father, she noticed something strange: her father's head was resting on the chair at the side of the bed.[15]

We may consider our lives mundane and our difficulties not worth sharing, but as a practice, Teresa suggests that we trust that Jesus is interested in whatever preoccupies us and that his eyes look with compassion on whatever we are doing. She invites us to link our feelings of sadness or joy with an event in Jesus' life that called forth a similar response from him. "If you are joyful, look at Him as risen. . . . If you are experiencing trials or are sad, behold Him on the way to the garden" (WP 26.4, 5). According to Teresa, Christ will be there for us no matter what our circumstances or daily preoccupations; we only need to glance in his direction.

To be sure, Teresa is not idealistic. She understands through her own experience how difficult it is to cultivate an intimate relationship with Christ when our attention tends to wander so easily. On the other hand, she is quick to remind us of what may be lost if we lose touch with this relationship, a lesson we may have learned too well from our own experience. As Christians, we are called to pray not occasionally but ceaselessly, Teresa insists. We are called to love God for God's own sake, not for something we can receive. We are called to be friends, not mere servants (John 15:15).

Do Not Hold Back

It is very important for any soul that practices prayer, whether little or much, not to hold itself back and stay in one corner.
(The Interior Castle, I.2.8)

Anyone who travels knows that you cannot hesitate or wander; you must keep moving. A seasoned traveler, in particular, knows how important it is to stay the course even in the midst of the rush and chaos of getting prepared and dealing with unexpected setbacks. If you want to reach your destination, you need a certain amount of discipline and focus or you will become more and more frustrated. Who has not found themselves searching for car keys or plane tickets at the last moment?

Teresa shows little patience for those who become complacent and drag their feet along the path of prayer. How, she asks, do they ever expect to get to the end of the road? The journey theme in Teresa's writings gives us a sense that we are "going somewhere,"writes the Carmelite author John Welch. "There is a destination to look forward to, and there is a way to that destination."[16]

As a result, the journey of prayer never loses momentum, even with our insecurities and setbacks, but continues with a certain rhythm. Recall that Jesus himself lived out of an ongoing rhythm of prayer, withdrawing from the crowds at times to be alone with his Father and then sharing this communion in his ministry.

Take the first step, Teresa advises, and then stop only to assess your situation and to make sure you are not lost because "it is very important for you to know that you are on the right road" (WP 22.3) Above all, do not settle for a plateau or opt for security. In fact, for Teresa, "there is no security in this life," so we must never abandon the path we are on (IC III.1.1).

Clearly, Teresa's encouragement to stay the course with prayer is a gift not only to her community but to us as well. She speaks to us as a guide who has traveled the path and knows its difficulties and rewards. Moreover, she addresses everyone on the prayer journey, from the beginner struggling with how to pray to those who are more advanced. She is well aware that we do not all receive the same grace, but she believes that we are all meant to be persons of prayer.

As we will see, Teresa is particularly supportive of those who are being called to transition from a meditative form of prayer—prayer that depends primarily on imagination and discursive reasoning—to prayer that is more contemplative. People at this stage in their journey, usually at midlife, are often confused by their experience, particularly if their prayer has become dry and difficult. What they need is assurance that their experience is temporary, a time of transition into deeper prayer. Teresa counsels, as always, perseverance and greater attentiveness to the call of love.

Give Your Entire Self to the Pilgrimage

Those who want to journey on this road and continue until they reach the end . . . must have a great and very resolute determination to persevere until reaching the end, come what may . . . even if they don't have courage for the trials that are met, or if the whole world collapses."
(The Way of Perfection, 21.2)

Teresa realized how easy it is to neglect the presence of divine love and fall into the trap of praying sporadically or not at all. Perhaps we make a concerted effort to pray during a retreat or during Lent, or maybe we resume a prayer discipline out of guilt, only to fall away again when the routine of life takes over. According to Teresa, to stop praying for any reason is to choose to be deaf to God's word.

If communication with God is not merely one activity among many others but the center from which all activity emerges, then it should be fundamental, the most important thing we do. The problem is that we tend to compartmentalize prayer, as another duty or responsibility that we fit into a busy day. Rather than being a heartfelt expression of gratitude, praise, or joy in response to God's loving presence in our lives, prayer is limited to times of need or to rote recitation during a ritual. Teresa asks us to see prayer not as a series of fitful stops and starts but rather as continuous, with times of rest and times of fertile growth—namely, a journey.

It is startling to see how little attention Teresa paid to methods and techniques of prayer. She desired one thing alone: to be present to divine love. Eventually, she found that awareness of God's presence infused all of her actions and became unceasing prayer, a tenet that is at the heart of the Carmelite rule.

The reality of the prayer journey will test our resolve to the core, Teresa assures us, and the destination will elude us. Distractions, lack of consolation, a sense of the absence of God—these will nag at us to the point that we may throw up our hands in frustration and eventually give up altogether. Teresa reminds us that as much as we would like to stay put, cocooned in our success, the prayer journey does not halt when we reach a certain stage. As pilgrims on earth, we are meant for ongoing transformation. We can no longer remain the person we once were because with each step, we are meant to awaken to greater self-knowledge.

Pilgrims must have absolute determination to persevere until reaching the end, "whether they arrive or whether they die on the road, or even if they don't have courage for the trials that are met" (WP 21.2). Although the pilgrim's path may be difficult and at times fraught with peril, Teresa's invitation and her insistence on staying the course speak to many today who ache to surrender completely to the pursuit of a pearl of great price. They are simply looking for encouragement to take the path seriously.

God addresses us now, says Teresa. If we want to hear what God is saying, we need to step aside from the noise of the world around us and let go of anything that prevents hearing, particularly our preoccupation with externals. Simply turn inward with faith and listen. At first you may hear only the chaos and confusion of your thoughts and be discouraged at the absence of any peace. However, be persistent and wait. God's voice is as subtle as the light breeze that causes a leaf to flutter in the forest stillness. If we are recollected—that is, fully attentive—we will hear it.

Let us now continue our preparation for the journey of prayer highlighted in the stages of the interior castle by exploring three virtues Teresa considered essential for growth in prayer: humility, self-knowledge, and detachment.

SUGGESTIONS FOR REFLECTION

1. Teresa invites us to look inward and keep moving on our spiritual journey. At what point in your life did you begin to take the interior journey seriously? What circumstances surrounded your movement inward at the time?

2. What prevents you from praying with the resolute determination to continue no matter what?

3. Is prayer food for the journey for you, nourishment for the soul? If not, what "food" are you substituting for it?

4. Teresa uses the image of the castle to describe the journey to the core of her being. Describe the image that appeals to you when you imagine organizing your life around a center.

5. As self-knowledge increases, you become more aware of your radical dependence on God. When have you come to know your dependence on an ultimate reality, and how did it change your sense of who you are?

CHAPTER TWO

Groundwork for Prayer

*Before I say anything about interior matters, that is,
about prayer, I shall mention some things that are necessary
for those who seek to follow the way of prayer; so necessary that
even if these persons are not very contemplative, they can be
far advanced in the service of the Lord if they possess these
things. And if they do not possess them, it is impossible
for them to be very contemplative.*

—The Way of Perfection, 4.3

Consider Marie, a young woman who was discouraged because her prayer life had dried up. For years she had set aside time daily to pray, write in her journal, and read spiritual literature that inspired her. Each year she attended a retreat and, for the most part, found the experience rejuvenating. However, her intuition told her that something was missing, and she realized that she had been losing touch with her relationship with God for some time. It was only after reflecting on the history of her prayer life (with the help of her spiritual director) that she appreciated how compartmentalized her prayer life had become, separate from her relationships and her daily life.

When Teresa wrote *The Way of Perfection*, a book meant to instruct those beginning the prayer journey, she dedicated the first chapters to how we should live and what attitudes we should have. This approach might surprise those who are expecting her to begin with a description of prayer forms or suggestions on how to pray.

Teresa believed that prayer needed times of solitude and silence. But just as important, it matures only when there is a connection between prayer and action. If the two are not interwoven, our relationship with God will suffer. She had no reservations about this approach: "It is necessary that your foundation consist of more than prayer and contemplation. If you do not strive for the virtues and practice them, you will always be dwarfs" (IC VII.4.9).

Many tend to think of prayer as removed from life or somehow above daily experience. If prayer is otherworldly, then our relationship with God has little to do with earthly concerns. As a result, we lose touch with our authentic self, our self in Christ, which is grounded in love. For this reason, Teresa cautions that we "shouldn't build castles in the air" (IC VII.4.15).

Come down to earth, she insists; let your relationship with God enter every corner of your life, even the mundane and difficult experiences. If you insist on segregating prayer, there will be consequences; prayer will become laborious and will eventually wither. Union with God is not possible, Teresa insists, "if we do not make the effort to gain the great virtues" (WP 16.6). The virtues she refers to are love, detachment, and humility.

Teresa's own reform convents provided every opportunity to integrate prayer and daily life. They were small, close-knit communities grounded in solitude and the spirit of poverty; they were also family environments that allowed human foibles to surface and, with these, the opportunity to deal with human weakness and develop friendship. Community life did not foster dour-faced contemplatives but rather nuns who laughed and enjoyed life, since prayer was balanced with time for recreation, communal prayer, and special feast days celebrated with flutes, drums, tambourines, and dance. Teresa would not tolerate a life of prayer that did not overflow into community life and keep alive a desire for God throughout the day.

Most important, Teresa avoided the temptation to cultivate love, detachment, and humility through the sheer power of the will. She believed that the practice of doing good and growing in virtue flows not from our efforts—as disciplined as these may be—but from our prayer. In our vulnerability and dependence, we hand ourselves over to grace and let prayer become "the basis for acquiring all the virtues" (WP 16.3). In time, as prayer deepens, the practice of virtues becomes easier.

There is no doubt that Teresa's approach to prayer contrasts strongly with our cultural belief in the efficacy of willpower. For example, we tend to get down on ourselves quickly when we fall short in our ability to love or in our lack of success in breaking a destructive habit.

As an antidote, Teresa reminds us that God alone is our source of strength, and prayer should be a stimulus for all good action. Growth in prayer naturally overflows into compassion for others and the desire to serve. Our attempt to take matters into our own hands will always lead to frustration since we are human and our human efforts repeatedly fall short. Humility, Teresa repeats; humility is essential for the journey.

With the Practice of These Three Things, Inner Peace

It is very important that we understand how much the practice of these three things helps us to possess inwardly and outwardly the peace our Lord recommended so highly to us. The first of these is

love for one another; the second is detachment from all created things; the third is true humility, which, even though I speak of it last, is the main practice and embraces all the others.
(The Way of Perfection, 4.4)

Teresa understands that love, detachment, and humility not only provide a necessary foundation for our prayer, but also introduce us to the deeper rhythms of meaning in our lives. In particular, as we grow in prayer, our eyes open to a wider horizon, and we become more self-aware and less self-absorbed—more attuned to the overall purpose and meaning of not only our lives but the lives of others. We also find an intimate connection between prayer and life itself, one flowing into the other and filling it with hidden potential.

Using the metaphor of her soul as a garden in which Christ takes a leisurely stroll, Teresa describes how important it is to open our hearts in prayer so that the Gardener of love will plant seeds of virtue (BL 14.9). Everything depends on the Gardener who weeds the garden, pulling up harmful growth—particularly those small sprouts that escape our attention. All of this tending creates space for growth and gives us the strength to love.

For Teresa, there is no room in the prayer journey to be self-absorbed or selfish because our lives should exhibit the virtues, particularly love, detachment, and, humility. Without these, prayer falters and growth in prayer becomes impossible. She considers these three virtues essential to a life of prayer because they offer us a way to identify with Christ's own humanity and give us the freedom to say yes to God's will for us.

Let us begin with love.

LOVING OTHERS

And be certain that the more advanced you see you are in love for your neighbor the more advanced you will be in the love of God, for the love His Majesty has for us is so great that to repay us for the love of neighbor He will in a thousand ways increase the love we have for Him. I cannot doubt this. (The Interior Castle, V.3.8)

Teresa had little patience with those whose prayer life prevented them from serving others. Like Christian mystics of all ages, she held that no matter what your spiritual discipline is, love is primary and the central point of the Christian message is charity. To separate yourself and not reach out to others would be the very opposite of what it means to be a Christian.

In *The Way of Perfection*, she was interested in giving practical advice to small reform communities in which "all must be friends, all must be loved, all must be held dear, all must be helped" (4.7). Later, though, in *The Interior Castle*, she writes more formally about the pursuit of perfect love. She describes "perfect" love not as an ideal unattainable for most, but rather as steady growth in these two things: love of God and love of neighbor.

Teresa warns that perfection in love does not mean coveting the feelings of warmth and reassurance that we may receive in prayer—as if we could cocoon our relationship with God—but, rather, expressing the love we have received in a way that benefits others. "For perfection as well as its reward does not consist in spiritual delights but in greater love and in deeds done with greater justice and truth" (IC III.2.10).

Teresa would give us this advice: tend to the sick, help ease the pain of others, and forget about what feelings you are trying to perpetuate in your prayer. As she wrote, "Works are what the Lord wants!" (IC V.3.11). If prayer does not overflow in a deepening love for God and neighbor, it is sterile because authentic prayer reveals itself in compassion. Teresa's emphasis on this truth is even more impressive when we recall that her own visions and ecstatic experiences did not impede her service to her community.

The best expression of love, Teresa tells us, is concrete, down-to-earth, and incarnational—in other words, not simply wishing someone well, but showing up on that person's doorstep to help. The quality of your help makes a difference: what is your intent when you reach out? She offers a homey suggestion: "Another very good proof of love is that you strive in household duties to relieve others of work, and also rejoice and praise the Lord very much for any increase you see in their virtues" (WP 7.9). Whether you are successful or not in your attempt to love is not primary because "everything done with a pure intention is perfect love" (7.7).

We may not be confident in our love for God, says Teresa, but be assured that when your love takes form through acts of compassion toward others, these are "strong indications for recognizing that we do love Him" (IC V.3.8). These words reassure those who tend to question their love for God and are looking for some tangible indication of its strength.

Teresa did not let her role as leader prevent her from taking up a dustpan and brush. She also grew in both love and humility toward her fellow nuns, frequently asking them to forgive her faults. In her midsixties, when she was renowned as the leader of the reform movement, she wrote to one of her prioresses about a change in her perspective on leadership: "You know, I no longer govern the way I used to. Love does everything. I am not sure if that is because no one gives me cause to reprove her, or because I have discovered that things go better that way."[17]

Teresa had little patience for those who criticized others or were judgmental. It was vitally important for her that we see the good in others and keep our own faults before our eyes. We should not spend our time focusing on the shortcomings of others but, rather, keep our own limitations in mind. How can we judge what is in someone else's heart? As a matter of fact, those whom we might think of as less important than ourselves, perhaps due to their lack of education or because of their family background, may have much to teach us. "We could truly learn from the one who shocks us what is most important even though we may surpass him in external composure and our way of dealing with others" (IC III.2.13).

Who has not had the experience of being tutored by someone we had written off as being less competent than we think we are? Perhaps, says Teresa, a good practice is to think of everyone as "better" than we are. In the end, "the safe path for the soul that practices prayer will be not to bother about anything or anyone and to pay attention to itself and to pleasing God" (BL 13.10).

In addition, Teresa counsels against being concerned about whether we are loved or not. She finds that in the long run, this concern for self fatigues the soul and can become harmful. When someone extends an expression of love toward us, we should show them that we are grateful and recognize that "the love comes from Him" (WP 6.5). In other words, we should practice following all the rivulets of love back to their source in God, and we will find peace.

Teresa was not idealistic. She knew change in our capacity to love is slow—a lifetime journey, in fact. Ultimately, we should not take our own efforts too seriously but count on God to perfect our love in God's own time. The important thing is that we continue to grow in love and not allow ourselves to become complacent. "I hold that love, where present, cannot possibly be content with remaining always the same" (IC VII.4.9).

Following Teresa's advice, we begin by not worrying about higher forms of love but focus on our natural inclination to serve others, particularly those in need, and reinforce this tendency. If we lack sensitivity to the needs of others, we practice reaching out in small ways. Let your prayer give you strength, says Teresa, and let your love flower into virtue. Growth in prayer will remind us how truly interconnected we all are.

DETACHMENT AS THE WAY TO FREEDOM

*Now let us talk about the detachment we ought to have,
for detachment, if it is practiced with perfection, includes
everything. I say it includes everything because if we embrace
the Creator and care not at all for the whole of creation,
His Majesty will infuse the virtues.*
(The Way of Perfection, 8.1)

Teresa links detachment and humility together. Both, she asserts, give us an awareness of our true state before God: that we are creatures, fully dependent on our Creator. This truth feeds our prayer and strengthens our relationship with God. Imagine a life of prayer in which you are aware of your complete dependence on God and desire to praise and thank God unceasingly for your very existence.

Perhaps a fuller realization of our dependence will come only through a radical change in our perspective. Sr. Mary Funk, a Benedictine nun, was visiting missionary friends in Bolivia when, during the course of an ordinary trip, she and her companions—three nuns, a priest, and a disabled boy—were swept away in a flash flood. She and the priest were the only survivors. Reflecting on her experience, she writes:

> That night in Bolivia, I never felt more mortal, or so aware of my need for salvation. It's an awareness I've never lost. Because I knew I couldn't have survived by my will alone, or even through the assistance of other people, but only through God, I felt my precariousness. . . . In other words, every day I recognize that I've been saved, and every day I know how much I need to be saved.[18]

For Sr. Mary Funk, salvation is not relegated to the future but occurs each moment of each day; we are always being saved, always being surprised by God's exorbitant love.

Keeping in mind this need to realize our complete dependence on God, we can turn to what Teresa means by "detachment." As knowledge and love of God grow in prayer, so does the desire to release attachments, to relax our grip on life, resulting in more room for this love.

For Teresa, the practice of detachment did not mean denying the importance of our relationships with people and possessions but rather bringing these relationships back into balance. When these relationships are allowed to assume undue importance, they usurp the centrality of divine love and hold us captive. Releasing our grip on attachments restores a balanced relationship and removes the heart from its self-made prison, freeing it to love God.

For example, Teresa was aware of the harm brought on by an attachment to honor, which, in the Spanish culture of her time, gave a person weight and worth in society. "God deliver us from persons who are concerned about honor while trying to serve Him" (WP 12.7). In her autobiography, she reflects on an ideal world in which monarchs, models for the people, could set aside their own honor and security and instead seek honor in God. As an option to an exaggerated allegiance to honor, she offers the possibility of a loyal friendship between equals. Since God has made us friends, we should overlook social standards and be friends with all (BL 21.2-3).

Teresa believed that any importance we have is not due to ourselves but comes from God. The need to save face, to feel important in front of others—as if our own honor and God's honor are the same—is absurd. She insisted that no one will grow spiritually if they continue to hang on to their self-importance. "Let any person who wants to advance and yet feels concerned about some point of honor believe me and strive to overcome this attachment, which is like a chain that cannot be broken by any file but only by God through our prayer and earnest cooperation. It seems to me that such attachment is a shackle on this road—I am astonished at the harm it does" (BL 31.20).

Reflecting on our own lives, we might consider how easy it is, if we have more, to separate ourselves from those who have little, or how quickly we respond to the sting of criticism, or how hurt we feel when we are not recognized.

DOING LITTLE BY LITTLE

Doing little by little what we can, we will have hardly anything else to fight against; it is the Lord who in our defense takes up the battle. (The Way of Perfection, 8.1)

Releasing ourselves from our attachments is not a matter of willpower and quick results but of allowing the love of God, which is nurtured in prayer, to guide us and give us strength little by little over a period of time. Without the guidance of love, detachment becomes an extension of our own agenda, even if it is spiritual.

However, Teresa warned her nuns that detachment is not easy even with the help of love; just because they had entered the convent and given up the world and outside relationships in answer to the call of love did not mean that their work was done. Teresa herself may have had in mind her early days in the convent, when in spite of being drawn to a relationship with God, she found herself attracted to the social pleasures of the parlor. Her experience reminds us that serious intent to love God does not prevent the will from being ensnarled by many things, even in the relatively safe confines of a religious community.

Teresa recognized that any attempt—even if it seems insignificant at the time—to preserve a self separate from God could lead to trouble. She offers her struggle with singing in the choir as an example. She was unfamiliar with the singing of the Office in community but did not ask for help for fear that others would see how lost she was. Once she realized the motivation behind her fear, she made it a point to approach the youngest member of the choir and ask for help. Her response shows how much care she took to stop the growth of self-interest even in small things.

One way Teresa remained alert to the pull of the ego was by recalling her mortality. She cultivated her reflections on death consistently from an early age and found that it gave her perspective on what was important. Her lifelong battle with illness certainly fueled this meditation. Mortality became her teacher, and in yielding to its mystery, she gained wisdom. "Teach us to count up the days that are ours, / and we shall come to the heart of wisdom" (Psalm 90:12). In the mirror of her finiteness, attachments no longer appeared as important, and her acts of self-centeredness wounded her deeply. She admitted, however, that even this practice of keeping death before one's eyes will not make it easy to put our desires aside because we "love ourselves greatly" (WP 10.2).

The weight that Teresa gives to detachment strikes a chord for us today. We are a pleasure-seeking culture that easily falls into cycles of addiction to drugs, food, busyness, consumerism, and more. As a child, I watched a TV that broadcast only a few channels and only in black and white. Today's numerous TV channels are hard to keep track of, and the Internet offers us further diversion with Facebook, blogs, and chat rooms. With such appealing and ever-present avenues for distraction and with such diverse ways of amusing ourselves, we easily forget to focus on the eternal, which gives our lives meaning and purpose. Teresa reminds us that there will be a time when entertainment and distractions will no longer feed a hungry soul but in fact constrict it. Usually at a time of loss, we become vulnerable enough to see that only in freedom will we find happiness.

Nothing More Important than Humility

While we are on this earth nothing is more important to us
than humility. . . . By pondering His humility, we shall see how
far we are from being humble. (The Interior Castle, I.2.9)

While on vacation at the Atlantic shore, I began to photograph feathers I had found. Some were lying on the sand glistening in the sunlight, while others were trapped in high sea grass and still others had been suddenly tossed and carried by a gust of wind and were dancing down the shoreline. Some feathers remained whole while others were tattered and torn due to their travels. I was attracted by their inherent fragility and their vulnerability to the environment. Unlike rocks and shells with their hard encasements, feathers are almost ephemeral and bring to mind the beauty and transience of all life, including my own.

Teresa knew that humility allows us to stay in touch with the truth that as contingent beings, we are radically dependent on the Creator. Like slender quills carried by the wind on a journey into the unknown, we need to keep in mind that our ultimate dependence is on God. This awareness is true self-knowledge, says Teresa, and should never be forgotten.

At every stage of spiritual development, Teresa emphasizes that growth in self-knowledge is only possible through humility. There will be a stage in our development when we will be tempted to sit back and relax, thinking that we have arrived. What people lack at this juncture, Teresa observes, is self-knowledge gained through humility. She warns that without humility, "we will remain here [at this stage] our whole life" (IC III.2.9).

How do we gauge our humility? Turn and face the tremendous mystery of God. God is the transcendent other, the very source of who I am. Reading the psalms, we find this perspective again and again.

> Look, you have given me but a hand's breadth or two
> > of life. . . .
> Every human being that stands on earth is a mere puff of
> > wind. . . .
> So now, Lord, what am I to hope for?
> My hope is in you. . . .
> I keep silence, I speak no more.
> (Psalm 39:5, 7, 9)

For Teresa, anyone who has not stood in wonder and awe before God and the mysteries of the world is not ready to encounter Jesus Christ. Only the vulnerability that comes from a deepening humility allows us to experience the helplessness of realizing that God reveals his own self in Jesus Christ.

Look at the events in Christ's life, suggests Teresa, and you will find a door into the inner life of God and into your own life. See his humility in comparison to your own; measure your actions only in relation to Christ, not in relation to anyone else.

In the light of Christ, who is Truth, our deceit and illusion become all too clear. By truth, Teresa refers not to a body of knowledge, rules on how to live, or a doctrinal concept, but rather truth as the reality of God who grounds all existence and who entered human history in Jesus. If we are to model Christ's humility, we need to release our self-conscious grip on life and, not holding anything back, put ourselves completely in God's hands, humbling ourselves as Christ did.

> [Christ], being in the form of God,
> did not count equality with God
> something to be grasped.
> But he emptied himself,
> taking the form of a slave,
> becoming as human beings are.
> (Philippians 2:6-7)

PRAYER IS BASED ON HUMILITY

What I have come to understand is that this
whole groundwork of prayer is based on humility
and that the more a soul lowers itself
in prayer the more God raises it up.
(The Book of Her Life, 22.11)

Never forget who you are before God, Teresa reminds us. Always remember that you are nothing in yourself; you receive your being entirely from God. This self-knowledge does not occur at once but grows over the years. As it does, it changes the way we see everything. We see everything as a gift and we see the divine presence in everything—in all creatures and in all of creation.

Teresa repeatedly refers to her own nothingness in her writings, and this may be off-putting to the general reader. Does she have an excessive sense of guilt, or is this reference a sign of her growing intimacy with God? It would be too easy to misinterpret her attitude as the extreme self-negation of a saint. In fact, in the context of all her writings, it is evident that as she drew nearer to God, she became aware of her limitations in light of the fullness and mystery of divine reality. In this light, the moral faults of her past life loomed large and seemed like the most horrible of evils. "By gazing at His grandeur, we get in touch with our own lowliness; . . . by pondering His humility, we shall see how far we are from being humble" (IC I.2.9). As a result, she acknowledged her inadequacies and complete dependency on God's mercy in a way that may seem extreme to us but that, in her eyes, fit her experience.

We can understand something of Teresa's perspective when we suddenly become aware of our own mixed motives. Even a loving action on our part can carry the residue of ego. We may think that we are doing God's will, but in reality, we repeatedly fall short. We need to accept the impurity of our motives and see ourselves as we are, not the selfless person we had imagined. We are helpless and dependent on God who, we now realize, must do everything for us. We surrender our autonomy as best we can, knowing that only in God will it be possible to find true freedom.

No wonder we find prayer so difficult and discouraging; it grows best when cultivated in humble conditions. According to ancient Italian folklore, an olive tree needs five things to flourish: drought, rocky soil, heat, solitude, and silence. According to Teresa, prayer comes alive when we embrace the challenging environment of the cross.

Deep prayer always strips us of what we think is important and offers no payoff; it teaches us how to do God's will. In the spirit of Teresa, Thomas Merton writes, "All our meditation should begin with the realization of our nothingness and helplessness in the presence of God. This need not be a mournful or discouraging experience. On the contrary, it can be deeply tranquil and joyful since it brings us in direct contact with the source of all joy and life."[19] Both mystics counsel that if our prayer dries up and we have no desire to continue praying, perhaps we have not been serious about seeking our true condition before God. To go into prayer with an awareness of our brokenness and our failures is a blessing that affirms our humanity and leads us into the depths of God's love.

Today we are encouraged to be aggressive, seek prestige, and strive for perfection at all cost. It is not surprising that the word "humility" rings hollow and evokes images of servitude or a negative and powerless self-image. However, for Teresa, humility does not distort our self-image but gives it rootedness in reality; it means having a true sense of who we are. It allows us to understand ourselves, both in our brokenness and sinfulness, but also in our dignity and giftedness as human beings.

With this fundamental sense of self, we are no better and no worse than others. Why compare ourselves to others, asks Teresa? Why boast? In reality we are nothing, completely dependent on Another. To recognize this is to know the truth but also to know true communion with God and with others, because we no longer see ourselves as separate or in competition. In particular, we gain the gift of compassion, accepting both our own limitations and the limitations of others.

Like a Bee Making Honey in a Beehive

For humility, like the bee making honey in the beehive, is always at work. Without it, everything goes wrong.

But let's remember that the bee doesn't fail to leave the beehive
and fly about gathering nectar from the flowers.
So it is with the soul in the room of self-knowledge.
(The Interior Castle, I.2.8)

Recall a time when your heart broke open, perhaps during a loss or a series of losses: illness, divorce, a family crisis, a transition time, or an inner upheaval. You may have thought of yourself as independent, secure, and able to handle the vagaries of your life, but this experience shook you to the core and made you aware of your vulnerability. At the time, the pain was overwhelming and blurred your vision; perhaps later, looking back, you were able to see this crisis as a real gift because it made you aware of a deeper sense of meaning and awakened you to humility.

Teresa says we have a choice: either we refuse to cultivate the seed of humility, perpetuating the illusion that we do not need God, or we can open our hearts to true self-knowledge and help our inner life flourish like bees in a hive. Instead of becoming solemn or downcast in spirit, we can experience an abundance of nectar, the outpouring of joy and deep gratitude. Not a passing feeling, this joy endures even when we are tested in the midst of difficult circumstances. Teresa had no patience with spiritual seekers who wore long faces and took themselves too seriously. She believed that joy was infectious and should radiate through her reform communities, inviting others to her doorstep.

The real secret of humility is that it opens the heart, heals it, and clears a path into the depths of our souls, releasing energy so that we can act freely and love without limits. How else could Teresa have continued her reform without the energy, strength, and depth of compassion that she received from humility? It was her complete dependence on God's grace as the source of all her gifts that gave her the strength to do whatever was needed and to act with a joyful spirit. According to Teresa, a good deal of our unhappiness results from living an illusion, living in the shadows rather than stepping into the beam of light that reveals the true self.

In humility we can acknowledge our dependence on the Spirit for the breath of our lives and address God with Teresa:

Do You see my heart here?
I place it in Your palm. . . .

I am Yours; for You I was born.
What do You wish to make of me? (P 7)

TELLING STORIES

I have recounted all this at length . . . so that the mercy
of God and my ingratitude might be seen; also, in order that
one might understand the great good God does for a soul that
willingly disposes itself for the practice of prayer.
(The Book of Her Life, 8.4)

As prayer matures in concert with the love, detachment, and humility, we discover a new perspective on our lives: our attention shifts away from a focus on failings and successes and turns to the story of God's mercy and love. It is no longer our search for God that matters but God's passionate desire for us. Our lives are not our own but rather the history of God's work in and through us.

When Teresa read St. Augustine's *Confessions* as a young nun, she discovered a story that resonated with her own. She identified with Augustine's conversion and was inspired to move beyond her struggle to integrate intimacy with God and her independent sense of self. Looking back on his own conversion, Augustine recognized his restlessness, frustration, and confusion, and cried out, "Late have I loved Thee, O Beauty so ancient and so new; late have I loved Thee!"[20] He saw that it was not his search for God that was primary, as he once thought, but rather God seeking him from within himself. Teresa, too, at the midpoint of her life, came to the conclusion that God had been present all the time drawing her toward intimacy, not as someone outside herself, but as the very source of her own searching.

In her autobiography, written at the request of her confessor, Teresa regrets the mistakes of her early years in the convent but recognizes that under the surface of these events, God's mercy was continually present: "In whom, Lord, can your mercies shine as they do in me who have so darkened with my evil deeds the wonderful favors You began to grant me?" (BL 4.4)

In chapters 10–40 of *The Book of Her Life*, Teresa describes a dramatic turn in her story. She writes, "This is another, new book from here on—I mean another, new life. The life dealt with up to this point was mine; the one I lived from the point where I began to explain these things about prayer is the one God lived in me" (BL 23.1). In the year 1554, she experienced a radical shift in consciousness as well as a heightened relationship with God in prayer. The first half of her life, she felt, was centered on her own point of view; the second half told the story of God's life within her. Teresa could now say with Paul, "It is no longer I, but Christ living in me" (Galatians 2:20).

We may not receive the unique outpouring of divine grace that Teresa experienced, but like her, we may find that in the telling of our own stories, we discover signs that our lives are not our own and that we are simply participating in God's work through us. Our stories become testimonies to grace. Even the insignificant events of everyday life, upon reflection, can reveal themselves as grace poured out into our lives. I believe that those who are given a chance to share even a part of their own life story will, in the telling, uncover a depth they did not expect.

In class I give each student an opportunity to stand in front of the group and share a meditation. They take a few lines from Scripture or from the text we are studying, reflect on it from the perspective of their own life experience, and close with a short prayer. This practice introduces them to a form of *lectio divina*. As might be expected, the students, including those who profess no faith, unexpectedly find themselves sharing a depth of meaning in their lives that may have been previously hidden from their conscious awareness. Offering their experiences to the group gives them the opportunity to claim their own life story.

For most, the short prayer that concludes the meditation flows from the heart. Even those who feel they will have difficulty with the prayer find that the words simply come to them. As might be expected, as the weeks progress, the sharing encourages a sense of community among the students because they realize how much the stories they have shared reflect one another.

One of the lessons I took from this classroom prayer was the power of story. Tales of healing, courage in the face of setbacks, and unexpected loss became an opportunity to share inner growth and the invitation to personal transformation. Each story seemed to mirror the one that preceded it. Theologian

Frederick Buechner points to the value of our personal stories as reflections of the stories of others and adds, "Maybe nothing is more important than that we keep track, you and I, of these stories of who we are . . . because it is precisely through these stories in all their particularity . . . that God makes himself known to each of us most powerfully and most personally."[21]

As spiritual seekers, we don't think we are capable of intimacy with God because we are not up to the demands of the relationship. "Who, me? How do I even imagine surrendering myself completely into God's hands when I am so mired in my sinful life?" Teresa addresses us, acknowledging our fear but at the same time assuring us that our trust in God's love will give us the courage that we need to pursue a more intimate relationship: "By considering the love He bore me, I regained my courage, for I never lost confidence in His mercy; in myself, I lost it many times" (BL 9.7).

She reminds us that in the end, it is not our effort but God's mercy that carries the day; our history is not our own. We learn through prayer to trust God more, to look with hope to the future, and to let the Spirit guide us.

Having explored the foundation of our prayer life—namely, love, detachment, and humility—we now turn our attention to the guidance Teresa offers us in *The Interior Castle*. Teresa envisions the human soul as an extraordinarily beautiful castle in which God dwells at the center. God continually invites us who are waiting outside to enter and find a home in truth and love. Those who choose to enter and explore the castle will pass through innumerable rooms toward greater knowledge of self and, at the same time, knowledge of God.

SUGGESTIONS FOR REFLECTION

1. Which virtues, or qualities of the heart, do you see growing and affecting your daily life because of your prayer?

2. Teresa sought to nurture authentic loving relationships in her reform communities. In what way have you witnessed or participated in the growth of mutual love in a community—family, church, group of friends—and what have you learned from the experience?

3. If you were to write the story of your life, how would you begin? What would be the most memorable turning point? When did you recognize that your life story is not about you but about God's mercy and love? How did this revelation change your outlook?

4. Teresa emphasized that God is truth itself, and to be humble is to live in this truth—in other words, to live with the awareness that we are nothing in and of ourselves. How has this truth entered your life? Has it made you downcast or joyful? Why?

CHAPTER THREE

Beginning to Pray: The Struggle

*It is a shame and unfortunate that through our own fault we
don't understand ourselves or know who we are.*
—*The Interior Castle, I.1.2*

Teresa makes it clear that beginning a relationship with God is difficult and that we have a deep resistance to any intimacy with divine love. We tend to run for the door at the slightest hint that we are loved unconditionally. As a result, the rooms of the first two dwellings of the "beautiful and delightful castle" (IC I.1.5) that is the soul introduce us to human weakness and self-constructed barriers that prevent intimacy. However, they also encourage us by revealing the gifts that await us if we take the journey seriously.

Teresa tells us that our soul exceeds in beauty and understanding anything we can say about it. She wants to impress upon us that whatever our definition of the soul is, it should be dismissed because "our intellects, however keen, can hardly comprehend it, just as they cannot comprehend God" (IC I.1.1). The soul cannot be limited because it is the presence of God within us. We can almost hear Teresa's enthusiasm as she reminds us that we were created in the image and likeness of God, and beyond anything we could expect, we have the potential to commune with God.

THE FIRST DWELLING PLACES:
THOUGH INVOLVED IN THE WORLD,
THEY HAVE GOOD DESIRES

For even though they are very involved in the world,
they have good desires and sometimes, though only once in a
while, they entrust themselves to our Lord and reflect on
who they are, although in a rather hurried fashion.
(The Interior Castle, I.1.8)

Those who inhabit the rooms of the first dwelling have good intentions to change their lives, but they continue to be pulled outward toward the periphery, where all the distractions await them. They focus on the business of making a living and protecting, as well as cultivating, a self-image. As a result, prayer is compartmentalized, one of several activities, and is filled with distractions and preoccupations. How do we listen to God when there is no real commitment to the journey and the thought of being in God's presence elicits fear? Teresa cuts through our rationalizations and excuses by insisting that our fear and hesitancy come from a lack of self-knowledge.

Beginners in prayer find themselves so enmeshed in the pursuit of worldly interests that these attachments—"reptiles," as she calls them, conjuring an image of horror and revulsion buried deep in our brains—have become their primary concern. As a result, instead of allowing themselves to be drawn inward toward their true identity in God, who is the treasure of the heart (Matthew 6:21), they succumb to an outward force that carries them away from the center. They do realize, however, that by finding their motivation in externals rather than in a deeper truth, they sacrifice self-knowledge, but they are too preoccupied to do anything about it.

Because so many "reptiles" get into these first rooms, it is difficult to find inner peace or be aware of the beauty of the castle. The "reptiles" (attachments) become layers of darkness that effectively block the experience of light and warmth that radiates from the center. In fact, any experience of light and warmth is so removed that it seems unreal.

Do you consider yourself more advanced in prayer than the people in these rooms and therefore find it difficult to identify with them? Teresa warns that there are many who fall back into these rooms because, through their own carelessness, they allow themselves to return to old habits and attachments. Be alert, she says, because the temptation to regress is strong, particularly in these first dwellings: "Guard yourselves . . . from extraneous cares" (IC I.2.15).

Those who allow distractions to waylay their attention and choose to stop praying or do not pray at all become paralyzed, like those who possess limbs but are unable to use them. These are people "so accustomed to being involved in external matters that there is no remedy, nor does it seem they can enter within themselves" (IC I.1.6). In other words, they have the capacity to listen to the call of love addressing them but choose to remain deaf. Because they stop praying, they drift into isolation from God and into a self-constructed hell.

How, then, should we characterize those who reside in these rooms? They make an effort to avoid serious sin and are willing to reflect on their lives occasionally and for brief periods.

Perhaps most important, they have awakened to a longing for God. It is this longing that draws them homeward to the center of the castle, if they trust it. These rooms, says Teresa, are meant for growth in humility and self-knowledge. She advises that we spend all the time that we need here rather than pushing forward. The key is to learn to turn our gaze toward God, because in knowing God's love, we realize how truly dependent we are.

Do I really need God? What is the treasure of my heart? How do I go about centering my life around God who resides in my inmost self? These questions indicate an intent to change, but as Teresa is quick to remind us, we are not in control; we will not be able to reclaim God as our center through our own efforts. Though we participate in the work of the Spirit, only God can reorient our hearts. We need to get out of the way and give God room to work. This process will not occur overnight but is a journey that takes a lifetime, and the impetus for the journey begins with wholehearted surrender.

PREPARING OURSELVES WITH FIRM RESOLUTION

The whole aim of any person who is beginning prayer—and don't forget this, because it is very important—should be that he work and prepare himself with determination and every possible effort to bring his will into conformity with God's will.
(The Interior Castle, II.1.8)

For all who embark on the prayer journey, whether beginners or those returning after a period of absence, Teresa stresses the need to be determined and persevere. God reaches out to us, and we must accept the invitation of divine love in the spirit of collaboration, which means determination and perseverance on our part. As Teresa puts it, "To those who want to journey on this road and continue until they reach the end, . . . I say that how they are to begin is very important—in fact, all important. They must have a great and very resolute determination to persevere" (WP 21.2).

Teresa says we need to be fearless and possess the courage of soldiers going into battle because we are engaging in spiritual warfare. Without this steadfast resolve, she believes there will be no success. When the disciples were overwhelmed by a riotous sea, Jesus told them not to fear but to trust (Matthew 8:24-26). In Teresa's imagination, the sea is churning all around us, threatening to take us off course and lessen our conviction to trust.

The power of external voices vying for the attention of the beginner cannot easily be dismissed. It is like trying to listen to yourself in a room filled with chatter; you are pulled constantly in one direction or another until you become immersed in the chaotic environment. In the same way, the general cultural discourse becomes so loud that we need the courage to step aside and listen to the voice of love within us. Instead of letting external voices have influence over us, we hold on to that inner voice with all our strength and never release it again. This is a key insight for Teresa.

Of course, translating this resolve into everyday life does not mean lessening our attention to work or family but, rather, integrating a spiritual discipline that will allow us to hear and respond to this call of love as it arises in the midst of our lives. Nevertheless, our spiritual practice may still seem daunting given our crowded and noisy lives. Teresa reminds us that it is only in welcoming the difficulty that we will uncover the kingdom within us: "If anyone wants to be a follower of mine, let him renounce himself and take up his cross and follow me" (Matthew 16:24).

Inevitably, we lose focus. The healthy eye becomes unhealthy (Matthew 6:22) because our souls "are still absorbed in the world and engulfed in their pleasures and vanities, with their honors and pretenses" (IC I.2.12). Our intentions may be good, but we are weak. Like any good spiritual director, Teresa suggests that we not despair but take our missteps as opportunities to turn to God for strength again and again. She followed this advice herself and heard these words of encouragement: "Do not fear, daughter; for I am, and I will not abandon you; do not fear" (BL 25.18).

Why not, then, take time on a regular basis to be with Jesus and draw close to him? Regularity is more important than the amount of time spent. What we say or how we pass the time is not as significant as the gift of our time. Time set aside for God is time not dedicated to ourselves.

Prayer is primarily a handing over of self. There are no set rules to follow; we simply align ourselves with our hearts' deep desire to love God and let this love be our guide. Then we make an effort to remember this loving presence throughout the day, using an image or prayer to anchor our attention.

Even when prayer becomes difficult and dry, persevere, advises Teresa. Rather than lose heart because we no longer receive the same reinforcing feelings that we once did, she suggests that we enter the desert and let the experience of dryness wash over us. In other words, let the desert teach steadfastness and courage and remind us of the necessity of turning our attention away from ourselves and toward God.

Eventually, our steadfastness will be rewarded, Teresa assures us: "A great treasure is gained by traveling this road; no wonder we have to pay what seems to us a high price" (WP 21.1). The call of love will center us and lessen the appeal of other interests that once held our attention. The time will come when we will understand how unimportant everything is next to so precious a treasure. Of what significance are our plans, goals, and attempts to prop up a self-image when held up against the light of eternity?

In the end, we find ourselves increasingly free to do the will of God and to receive what has been promised (Hebrews 10:36). Determination and perseverance win the day. For Teresa, the trials and tribulations experienced along this road, as difficult as they are, offer a great gift—namely, the emergence of new life in God.

THE SECOND DWELLING PLACES: LISTENING TO A MORE PERSONAL CALL

These rooms, in part, involve much more effort than do the first, even though there is not as much danger, for it now seems that souls in them recognize the dangers, and there is great hope they will enter further into the castle. (The Interior Castle, II.1.2)

Those in the rooms of the second dwelling have begun to pray more consistently and listen more attentively to the call of love. The inner journey begins in earnest. The ear of the heart has become more attuned to God's voice and more inclined to take a deep look at the soul.

Prayer is also more honest and open; we find ourselves facing the truth of our lives with nowhere to hide. The psyche releases material from the depths of the unconscious, dark secrets that have been closeted due to shame or fear. The truth penetrates the caverns of the heart with such laser-like intensity that it makes us fearful. Who wants to face the Truth when it is so simple and direct? We stand before God as fragile and broken human beings in need of divine mercy.

Because prayer is so emotionally honest, we look for ways of avoiding it, at times unaware of our escapism. Teresa admits that there were times when she would have rather performed any penance than pray because she found prayer so painful: "For some years, I was more anxious that the hour I had determined to spend in prayer be over than I was to remain there" (BL 8.7)

The bottom line, however, is that those who inhabit these rooms lack determination to remain in them because they continue to put themselves in the occasions of sin. Such carelessness makes it easy to fall backwards. Nevertheless, on the positive side, Teresa tells us that we are gaining a heightened awareness of dangerous situations and are more convinced of the importance of avoiding them.

Perhaps the greatest change in this dwelling is that God's call is now experienced as personal. We are told that "every hair on your head has been counted" (Luke 12:7). The call was previously experienced in a general, even vague way, but now it is addressed to me in my unique history and in a tone that I cannot ignore. Hearing the voice of One who truly loves you call your name so intimately weighs heavy on the soul, says Teresa: "His voice is so sweet the poor soul dissolves" (IC II.1.2).

Also, God's profound graciousness becomes more evident. We realize that all along, divine Love has been seeking us relentlessly through life experiences: books, conversation, music, illness and crises, and times of prayer. Like the father of the prodigal son/daughter, our God has great patience and is willing to wait for us if we show perseverance and a heartfelt desire to return home.

More than ever, the temptation to retreat hounds us because we are more awake, more sensitive to God's call, and we realize how much there is to lose. Having gained some self-knowledge, we find ourselves invited to embrace a new story, a conversion. Or we can return to our familiar lives, immersing ourselves once again in the voices of the crowd. However, Teresa reminds us that returning to the periphery of life is no longer a viable option because we are haunted by this question: "What hope can we have of finding rest outside of ourselves if we cannot be at rest within" (IC II.1.9).

BLOWS FROM THE ARTILLERY STRIKE

The blows from the artillery strike in such a way that the soul cannot fail to hear. . . . And the afflictions of the poor soul: it doesn't know whether to continue or to return to the first room.
(The Interior Castle, II.1.3, 4)

Though we hear a call to ongoing conversion, we often do not have the strength to respond without hesitation. We find ourselves in the middle of a conflict, pulled into two directions. Double minded, our will is too weak to focus on one thing alone because we lack purity of heart.

Teresa tells us that there is a strong temptation to see earthly pleasures, comfort, and security as more important than they are, even eternal; we wonder how it is possible to let them go. Not long after his conversion, Thomas Merton realized that he was still hanging on to his past life; he imagined that he was a good Christian but knew that his heart was divided: "Where was my will? 'Where your treasure is, there will your heart be also.' . . . I wanted to enjoy all kinds of pleasures of the intellect and of the senses and in order to have these pleasures I did not hesitate to place myself in situations which I knew would end in spiritual disaster."[22]

The inner war becomes so intense that we are confused and do not know whether we should retreat or not. The narrow ego, or self, having been central for much of our lives, is holding its ground against the threat of an expansive self, the self in Christ. Teresa encourages "those who have begun, not to let the war make them turn back" (IC II.1.9).

Teresa became acutely aware of her own inner battle while caring for her dying father. She had told her father that she had stopped praying due to her prolonged illness, yet in truth she found a heartfelt turn inward difficult because her attention was rooted in numerous pleasures and concerns. Being present to her father at his bedside as he died unnerved her and caused her to reflect on her situation. "On the one hand God was calling me; on the other hand I was following the world. All the things of God made me happy; those of the world held me bound" (BL 7.17). Eventually, she confided her condition to her father's confessor, and he encouraged her to begin praying again, which she did and never stopped.

Though Teresa wished for a reprieve from the inner struggle, the conflict continued to rage within her and even intensified. She confessed that "for more than eighteen of the twenty-eight years since I began prayer, I suffered this battle and conflict between friendship with God and friendship with the world" (BL 8.3). She acknowledged that the turmoil should be expected. Prayer had uncovered the true self and, in doing so, exposed a lie: "I was living an extremely burdensome life, because in prayer I understood more clearly my faults" (7.17).

Because the inauthentic self passed for so long as her identity, she found it difficult to imagine letting go of it. Our attachments, says Teresa, do not fade but rather present themselves as essential to our lives. The light of God's love exposes our brokenness and alienation, not only from God, but from ourselves as well. She addresses God in this way: "How can I extol the favors You gave me during these years! And how at the time when I offended You most You quickly prepared me with an extraordinary repentance to taste Your favors and gifts!" (BL 7.19).

Sadly, Teresa sought help during her struggle but suffered at the hands of many confessors who were misguided. However, she encourages us to find support from "persons with experience" (IC II.1.10). She suggests that spiritual directors who have walked the path and can speak from their experience would be ideal, but if they are not available, we should trust that "the Lord will guide everything for our benefit" (II.1.10).

Don't Be Discouraged

If you should at times fall don't become discouraged and stop striving to advance. For even from this fall God will draw out good. (The Interior Castle, II.1.9)

Confronted by the temptation to be relieved of the tension, those who inhabit these rooms may return to the false security of their former lives and not deal with this central question: "Who am I?" This question evokes fear and restlessness because it invites us to claim our true identity and answer the call to intimacy that arises from our deepest self, our inner truth. At this stage, we realize that this call cannot be dismissed as one concern among many but that it goes to the heart of who we are. Teresa advises surrender to grace and prays, "Ah my Lord! Your help is necessary here; without it one can do nothing. In Your mercy do not consent to allow this soul to suffer deception and give up what was begun" (IC II.1.6).

There may be a tendency in the middle of this inner turmoil to take things into our own hands and push ahead even though we sense that we do not have the spiritual resources necessary. Teresa, however, counsels gentleness toward ourselves; rather than emphasizing self-will, she would have us depend on love and our growing relationship with God.

It is love that sets us free, not our willfulness. Willfulness makes prayer more difficult because the focus is on the self rather than on the work of the Holy Spirit. In the middle of a raging battle, release yourself to the love and mercy of God, counsels Teresa. Trust this relationship and realize that things will become overwhelming only when we forget it.

Teresa advises that we need to take time to reflect in order to see through the illusion. Remembering the signs of God's love in our lives will assure us that we will never be abandoned, and reminding ourselves that there is no security outside the castle walls allows the heart to be at peace. Teresa also warns us not to make consolations important in prayer and chides those who do so. They are still beginners on the path, she points out, and should not be complaining about what they think they deserve.

The path of prayer incorporates the way of the cross, Teresa reminds us. We should not let trials and setbacks discourage us, but instead, we should view them as an invitation to trust even more in the mercy of God.

For Teresa, the mystery of the cross gives meaning to our suffering, to the trials, turmoil, and tension we experience. She emphasizes that God gives the cross to intimate friends to share the path he walked and desired for himself. So if we want to grow in intimacy with God, we can expect that we will be refined in the crucible of suffering. As a result, we become strengthened, purified, and renewed, growing in our capacity for divine love. Teresa does not propose suffering for suffering's sake but suffering for love's sake, for love of God and others. Those who want to grow in love choose to suffer in union with the crucified Christ.

Whenever we suffer, we are given a cross to embrace, and this cross, says Teresa, becomes our prayer: "For if the soul is alert, I don't consider the suffering of illness and pain a problem, even though this may be a trial, for the soul is praising God and accepting this as coming from His hand" (F 29.3).

CULTIVATING A GARDEN ON BARREN SOIL

Beginners must realize that in order to give delight
to the Lord they are starting to cultivate a garden on
very barren soil, full of abominable weeds.
(The Book of Her Life, 11.6)

Gardeners know how difficult it is to establish a garden in a place where the soil is barren and weeds flourish. The digging and hoeing is hard work, and then the soil must be enriched, the seeds planted, and the growing plants tended. When my wife, Diana, and I created a garden out of the chaos of vegetation and uneven terrain, we took on the task with relish but soon recognized that we may have underestimated the project.

The days seemed endless, and the work, draining. The earth itself seemed to reject our efforts. Even today I can hear the cultivator moaning as it slowly clawed its way through soil as hard as clay. Looking at pictures of the project now, many years later, our bodies still ache.

When Teresa compares cultivating a garden on barren soil to the prayer of a beginner, she has my attention. Her image tells the story well. A beginner at prayer must engage in hard work for growth to take place. If the beginner puts in the time and labor, she says, then God, the Master Gardener, will respond. We till the earth, pull the weeds, and plant the seed, and with grace, the miracle of new life occurs. But it will not be easy.

You would think that Teresa would assure beginners that once the difficult labor is over, they will experience prayer that is easier and more enjoyable. After all, she goes through the trouble of outlining stages of growth in prayer that evolve around watering a garden. The first is the laborious task of drawing water from the well. The second, involving less work, depends on aqueducts to get the water to the plants. The third—easier yet—depends on rivers and streams. The last is prayer without effort on our part but completely dependent on the sheer grace of rain.

However, rather than focusing only on the joy of growth in prayer, Teresa explains that even as the beginner matures, the labor will not let up because "whether in the beginning, the middle, or the end, all bear their crosses even though these crosses be different" (BL 11.5). "Comfort" and "ease" are not in her vocabulary when it comes to prayer, though "joy" and "love" certainly are. Most, I suspect, would agree with her.

Her point is clear: from the beginning of the journey onward, prayer will always be tied to sacrifice because authentic love will always demand sacrifice. "For there are many who begin, yet they never reach the end. I believe this is due mainly to a failure to embrace the cross from the beginning" (BL 11.15). She knew this from personal experience because even as she grew in her prayer life, she had to integrate the rigors of convent discipline, the simple life of poverty, and the practice of humility, detachment, and charity into her prayer journey.

It seems that the medieval mystic Dame Julian of Norwich agrees with Teresa's emphasis, even drawing on the same image of gardening. In a personal revelation, Julian saw a servant standing respectfully before his lord:

> There was a treasure in the earth which the lord loved. . . . I watched, wondering what kind of labor it could be that the servant was to do. And then I understood that he was to do the greatest labor and the hardest work there is. He was to be a gardener, digging and ditching and sweating and turning the soil over and over, and to dig deep down, and to water the plants at the proper time. And he was to persevere in his work, and make sweet streams to run, and fine and plenteous fruit to grow.[23]

Julian identifies the servant as representing both Christ and each of us. Through his incarnation, passion, and death, Christ shows us the sacrifice necessary to be a gardener for the sake of love. We are to follow his example and walk in his footsteps.

Those who pray must dedicate themselves to the work of gardening the soul if they are to enjoy the fruits of their labor. However, this work of a good gardener does not sit well with a culture motivated toward ease and dispensation. For us, buying food from the local store is much easier than tending a garden in the hot sun and dealing with weeds and insects. Rather than using a watering can or hose, we prefer the convenience of an automatic sprinkler system.

What other difficulties will the gardener encounter in prayer? Beginners, in particular, will struggle mightily with distractions and find that bringing their attention back again and again requires great effort. They must also deal with the unloading of the unconscious that takes place as prayer deepens, particularly the reality of a past life and the painful memories of suffering and sinfulness. They will have to face their lack of contrition and the detours they took to avoid the truth. All these experiences weigh heavy on the spirit and certainly compare to the hard work of establishing a garden.

"These labors take their toll," admits Teresa. "Being myself one who endured them for many years . . . "(BL 11.11). But she is quick to add that God does not abandon us in our labor, and we will be repaid quite well for our effort. She reminds us, however, that in the end we should not fall into the ego trap of taking ourselves and our work too seriously, because ultimately everything depends on grace. Without grace, we could not even begin cultivating the garden of our soul.

Keep Jesus Present within You

I tried as hard as I could to keep Jesus Christ, our God and our Lord, present within me, and that was my way of prayer.
(The Book of Her Life, 4.7)

Through her study of one of her favorite books, Francisco de Osuna's *The Third Spiritual Alphabet*, Teresa discovered the importance of active recollection and emphasized it in the first through third dwellings of the castle. For Teresa, recollection occurs when "the soul collects its faculties together and enters within itself to be with its God" (WP 28.4). It is simply a heartfelt turn inward that we initiate.

It is helpful to think of recollection as moving beyond distractions, chatter, busyness, cell phones, computers, and constant noise in order to be present to our true self. Recollection does not remove us from the responsibility or enjoyment of our lives, but it means turning our heartfelt attention to the presence of God—not an easy practice in our hyperactive, technological culture.

By withdrawing from external things and gazing within ourselves, trusting that God is always near, we can be present to and converse with Christ. All that we need to do is "look at Him within oneself" and "speak to Him as to a father" (WP 28.2). Through this practice, says Teresa, we learn to speak with God about our trials, suffering, loss, and joy with the humility of a person who knows that in the end, all is well. This intimate sharing between friends invites further growth in our mindfulness of Christ.

Teresa's main concern for the prayer of recollection is simple: to live in the loving presence of Christ. She invites us to uncover a reality of God in us that puts all other realities in perspective. She acknowledges that though the Spirit of Christ is always present, we are not always aware of him, nor do we cultivate our awareness. Such forgetfulness cannot be taken lightly, however, because, as she stresses, "All the harm comes from not truly understanding that He is near" (WP 29.5). Our ongoing openness to Jesus' presence gives God room to work within our hearts and transform us more and more from self-interest to God-consciousness.

Teresa was not interested in methodical reflections and did not feel comfortable with extensive use of the imagination, but she did use meditation books and imagery, particularly scenes from the Gospels, to recollect herself: "I have always been fond of the words of the Gospels . . . and found more recollection in them than in very cleverly written books" (WP 21.3). She also loved to gaze at the beauty of nature and let it draw her into the presence of Christ, confessing that "it helped . . . to look at fields, or water, or flowers" (BL 9.5). She valued all forms of meditation because she felt they enkindled a desire for greater love and made us more dedicated to our spiritual journey. She also considered meditation a preparation for deeper prayer because it helped us ward off distracting thoughts. She preferred simple reflections and images of saints or of biblical events that she carried with her to turn her attention to Christ's presence.

When Teresa pondered one of the mysteries of Christ's life, her recollection was not as much an exercise of the imagination or reason as it was a gentle attention to a particular mystery that mirrored her present condition and drew her back into Christ's presence. For example, she often gravitated to Gethsemane: "The scene of His prayer in the garden, especially, was a comfort to me; I strove to be His companion there" (BL 9.4). This image became a window into her soul and, with grace, would open into the self-forgetfulness of deep prayer.

Teresa's practice of active recollection, particularly her attraction to certain scenes from Christ's life, reminds me of the monks' cells that I saw at the Dominican Monastery of San Marco in Florence. Each cell has a large fresco painted by the

Renaissance artist Fra Angelico on one of the walls. The subject for each fresco was taken from the life of Christ and was meant to be an ongoing reminder for the monk. Imagine the monk waking, fasting, praying, and sleeping in the company of this image for weeks, months, and years. The Gospel scene would soon become etched in his heart and spontaneously rise up in his awareness, reminding him of the presence of Christ, in the same way that a word or phrase like "Jesus" or "Come, Holy Spirit" could function as a mantra in a prayer of recollection, helping a person return to God when the mind strays.[24]

We can imitate Teresa's practice and the experience of the Dominican monks by choosing one scene from the Gospels that speaks to our heart at this time in our life. Reflect on how this scene mirrors your heart, and then recall the image throughout the day, briefly bringing it to mind as a way to remember that you walk in the presence of Christ. Attention to the presence of Christ within her was primary for Teresa, while the image was secondary.

SAYING ONE WORD OF THE OUR FATHER

Consider that you are losing a great treasure and that you do much more by saying one word of the Our Father from time to time than by rushing through the entire prayer many times.
(The Way of Perfection, 31.13)

For Teresa, once we have moved within and recollected ourselves, simple vocal prayer can be extraordinarily powerful. Fixing your gaze on Christ, "represent the Lord Himself as close to you and behold how lovingly and humbly He is teaching you" (WP 26.1). Teresa does not consider it necessary to imagine or think of Christ, but just to gaze at him with the eyes of your heart and pray the Our Father.

Remaining attentive to God's presence is essential, says Teresa, because "a prayer in which a person is not aware of whom he is speaking to, what he is asking, who it is who is asking and of whom, I do not call prayer however much the lips move" (IC 1.7). She recognizes how easy it is to find ourselves saying the words in a singsong fashion without much attention or reverence to the One we are addressing. Distractions can be expected no matter what approach to prayer we choose, but by giving in to them, we lose attention.

Teresa preferred the Our Father because it is the prayer that Christ taught his apostles. No matter where we are in our journey, Teresa suggests, it is enough to say aloud or interiorly the Our Father. She explores the Lord's prayer with reverence and wonder in several chapters at the end of *The Way of Perfection*, reflecting the attitude of the early Christians who considered the prayer so important that only those who were baptized were allowed to recite it.

Echoing Teresa's concern for attentiveness, one spiritual writer notes that saying the Our Father with attention means "thoughtfully and concretely, savoring each phrase, allowing it to open the mind to God."[25] Teresa agrees that it is better to repeat one word of the Our Father than rush through it. At the same time, praying the Our Father assumes a posture of heart that we, with our preference for individualism, find difficult today; we are invited to bow before God and recognize our reliance on divine love and mercy. If we truly address our Father with an awareness of our complete dependence, then we will recognize that the prayer is not private, as many assume, but one that already includes God, self, and neighbor.

God will respond to our effort to say the Our Father with gentle loving attention, Teresa assures us: "Even though we may recite this prayer no more than once in an hour, we can be aware that we are with Him, of what we are asking Him, of His willingness to give to us, and how eagerly He remains with us. If we have this awareness, He doesn't want us to be breaking our heads trying to speak a great deal to Him" (WP 30.6).

Following Teresa's example, consider making a resolution to repeat the Our Father at least once a day. As we have seen, whether we recite the prayer orally or interiorly, it is fundamentally important to be present to God as completely as we are able. We begin with an awareness of our communion with God, self, and all other beings, and acknowledge our complete dependence on divine love for breath itself. Then we say the words slowly, perhaps linking them to the rhythm of our breath, all the while gazing at Jesus.

RAISED TO PERFECT CONTEMPLATION

I tell you that it is very possible that while you are reciting the Our Father or some other vocal prayer, the Lord may raise you to perfect contemplation.
(The Way of Perfection, 25.1)

In Teresa's time, prayer was artificially divided into categories, and vocal prayer in particular was thought to be unrelated to "higher" forms like contemplation. For Teresa, however, prayer is organic, one method of prayer feeding another. She tells us that simply saying the Our Father vocally can dispose a person to contemplative prayer: "I don't know how mental prayer can be separated from vocal prayer if the vocal prayer is to be recited well with an understanding of whom we are speaking to" (WP 24.6).

Teresa understands that both forms of prayer, vocal and contemplative, share a common ground—being mindful of whom you are addressing and allowing the Spirit to lead you into deeper inner silence. As we have seen, she calls this practice of wholehearted centering the path of recollection and assures us that we will see signs of growth. "If we make the effort, practice this recollection for some days, and get used to it, the gain will be clearly seen" (WP 28.7).

As an example, Teresa refers to a nun who was led to contemplation through her faithful recitation of the Our Father.

> I know a person who was never able to pray any way but vocally, and though she was tied to this form of prayer she experienced everything else. And if she didn't recite vocal prayer her mind wandered so much that she couldn't bear it. . . . Once she came to me very afflicted because she didn't know how to practice mental prayer nor could she contemplate; she could only pray vocally. I asked her how she was praying, and I saw that though she was tied to the Our Father she experienced pure contemplation. (WP 30.7)

We learn from Teresa that beyond method or technique, prayer is fundamentally our gaze of love toward Christ. Being aware of Christ's gaze and longing for us, we allow our desire for him to awaken. We remain in Christ's presence with a humble and open-hearted disposition throughout our prayer, whether it is the Our

Father or another form of recited prayer like a psalm. And we trust, with Teresa's assurance, that "it is very possible that while you are reciting the Our Father or some other vocal prayer, the Lord may raise you to perfect contemplation" (WP 25.1)

DO NOT BE DISTRESSED

It is very important that no one be distressed or afflicted over dryness or noisy and distracting thoughts.
(The Book of Her Life, 11.17)

One of Teresa's ongoing themes is that to take prayer seriously, we need to give time freely to Jesus and continue to persevere, no matter how we are feeling or what obstacles present themselves. Whether we are too busy, preoccupied, or experiencing difficulties, our most important concern should be our intention to be present and to give Christ our time and attention in the best way we are able. After all, we do not hesitate to set aside time with friends and family or take the opportunity to pursue our own interests.

Teresa reminds us too that difficulties can be expected for the beginner because our wills are not yet in conformity with God's will. We become discouraged because the gap between God's love for us and our love for God is so great that there seems to be little hope of bridging it. Yet if we remain true to our relationship with Christ, Teresa assures us, we will continue to grow and realize just how much we are loved.

Teresa adds that many beginners lose their way on the path of prayer because they pay too much attention to the warm feelings they receive when they should be concentrating on trusting what God desires for them. She makes her point with dry humor: "It's an amusing thing that even though we still have a thousand impediments and imperfections and our virtues have hardly begun to grow . . . , we are yet not ashamed to seek spiritual delights in prayer or to complain about dryness" (IC II.1.7).

She is not diminishing the importance of these consolations in prayer because they are a valuable support, but she warns that becoming attached to them may hinder growth. Perhaps, she suggests, times of frustration and the lack of feeling in prayer are times for the hidden maturation of the soul. In other words, as John of the Cross and Teresa both agree, the real spiritual work takes place hidden from us in darkness.

To worry about how much we are progressing or whether we are following the right routine is unnecessary. To focus on God's interest in everything we do is enough. As difficult as this is, we should ask ourselves, "Is this relationship transforming me ? Is my behavior changing, and are my actions more and more an expression of love?" In other words, am I integrating my relationship with God and his will into my life?

Teresa promises that as our intimacy with God grows and we learn to trust, we will uncover a surprising grace of unceasing prayer, the charism of the Carmelites and the gift that Teresa herself would most like us to experience.

No Need for Wings to Find Him

However softly we speak, He is near enough to hear us. Neither is there any need for wings to go to find Him. All one need do is go into solitude and look at Him within oneself, and not turn away from so good a Guest. (The Way of Perfection, 28.2)

What better way to nourish the prayer of recollection, a prayer that cultivates a contemplative openness to Christ's presence, than solitude? Teresa writes, "We must desire solitude. . . . This desire is continually present in souls that truly love God" (F 5.15). Beginners in prayer, in particular, she believed, should cultivate space in the heart for intimacy with the divine. How else are we to hear the soft whisper of love?

We can trace Teresa's passion for solitude and silence back to the original Carmelites on Mount Carmel. The image of a group of hermits immersed in solitude on a lonely mountain charged her imagination and motivated her to establish the practice of solitude and silence for the Carmelite community. She founded her reform monasteries around the ideal of solitude to facilitate the heart's listening, which overflows into ceaseless prayer. According to one commentator, "Key to Teresa's reform was her conviction that the Monastery of the Incarnation was too crowded and busy for solitude and contemplative prayer that she came to consider integral to Carmelite life."[26] In contrast to the large community and crowded conditions that she had experienced as a young nun, Teresa limited the numbers in her new foundations, allowing for ample solitude and silence in the context of a family-like atmosphere.

Even vocal prayer like the Our Father should be "recited in solitude," says Teresa, because this is what Jesus did (WP 24.4). She held that it is important to go within oneself and uncover the heart's solitude, not only in times of prayer, but even in the midst of activity. "We must . . . disengage ourselves from everything so as to approach God interiorly. . . . Although it may be for only a moment that I remember I have that Company within myself, doing so is very beneficial" (29.5). In this practice, we are simply turning our attention to the One whose gaze is always upon us and strengthening our awareness of God's nearness, no matter what the circumstances. As a result, we live our lives differently, open to deeper heart listening, which may lead to the gift of contemplation.

There are times when we simply need to go aside into solitude, like the prophet Hosea, not because we choose to, but because God calls us (Hosea 2:16). Of the souls in the second dwelling, Teresa says that "this Lord desires intensely that we love Him and seek His company, so much so that from time to time He calls us to draw near Him. And His voice is so sweet the poor soul dissolves at not doing immediately what He commands" (IC II.1.2). Our best response to this loving invitation to intimacy is the embrace of solitude and silence.

There is no doubt that even if we agree with Teresa's emphasis, the idea of solitude is radical for us today because it means creating a break in the flow of a busy and often chaotic day. Even the mention of solitude and silence causes us to squirm. How do I find room in my schedule? Isn't solitude for those who are introverts or who are more advanced on the spiritual path? What am I supposed to do with my time in solitude?

The problem is that we cannot be attentive to God and the world, says Teresa, without the ability to listen deeply. We can easily become lost in the cacophony that pervades daily living. However, by moving from activity to the stillness of solitude, we travel a pathway to recollection and openness to the Holy Spirit. At times, Teresa found solitude so refreshing that in spite of her gregarious personality, she had to withdraw from conversation: "Sometimes it gives me great pain to have to have dealings with others . . . because all my longing is to be alone" (T 1.6).

Most of all, we fear solitude, not because the dynamics of our day makes it inconvenient, but because the truth uncovered in solitude invites change. God pulls us aside into a crucible for the purpose of transformation and addresses us in ways that are unexpected.

Solitude effectively purifies the spirit and opens the heart to truth. Our initial response is to pack the tent and head for more familiar terrain. We would rather distract ourselves with chatter, TV, the Internet, or the hum of city life rather than face ourselves. However, if we learn how to wait, no matter how painful it is, solitude gives us a new perspective on our lives, grounds us in hope and love, and heightens our awareness of an inner peace.

Do you desire to listen to the voice of God? Cultivate silence and solitude because these give us the opportunity to remember the depths of the heart and be attentive: "Do you think He is silent? Even though we do not hear Him, He speaks well to the heart" (WP 24.5). Teresa reminds us that it is necessary "to be alone with Him alone" (BL 36.29).

SUGGESTIONS FOR REFLECTION

1. How have you struggled to listen to God? What has been your response to your difficulties in prayer?

2. What preoccupation—possessions, entertainment, busyness, work, among others—might have prevented you from going deeper in prayer in your life?

3. How has God been speaking to you personally? Through relationships, music, books, prayer, special places, illness, setbacks? Something else? How have you responded to this call?

4. What inner conflict may have caused you to be distant from God and prevented knowledge of your true self?

5. In what way has prayer uncovered the reality of who you are in the eyes of God?

> I, Yahweh, search the heart,
> test the motives,
> to give each person what his conduct
> and his actions deserve. (Jeremiah 17:10)

6. In solitude we discover the voice that has addressed us first and the One who has loved us before we expressed love to others. What have you discovered about your life in your own journey into solitude?

7. "How hard it is . . . to enter the kingdom of God!" Jesus tells us (Mark 10:23). Teresa emphasizes the need for strong determination. How have you nurtured this determination in your life so that you can set your heart on the kingdom of God's love?

CHAPTER FOUR

From Security to a More Contemplative Prayer

Let us speak now of those souls whose lives are so well ordered;
let us recognize what they do for God.
—*The Interior Castle*, III.1.7

Though the rooms of the first two dwellings of Teresa's castle may be difficult and demanding, they are a necessary portal for embarking on the journey into prayer. They introduce us to the reality of the inner life by teaching humility and self-knowledge, and they offer an invitation to a deeper encounter, which occurs in dwellings three and four, the focus of this chapter.

Those who arrive in the rooms of the third dwelling are mature Christians who have found stability in their faith and in their prayer and who lead disciplined lives. They have also learned to balance prayer with acts of charity. Not all is well, however, because they have certain expectations; for example, they depend on receiving satisfaction both from their prayer life and from their spiritual path in general. Teresa tells us that people in this dwelling can become too secure in their self-image as good Christians who are engaged in active ministry. She advises that it is time for them to release their attachment to their way of life and open their hearts to even greater freedom.

Teresa believed that if the people in the rooms of the third dwelling were willing to take the risk, release their need for control, and journey into the unknown, they would find themselves invited to contemplative prayer. These rooms represent a time of transition. They are characterized by our desire to listen intently to God's deeper call, a call that encourages less control and activity on our part and more detachment and receptivity. We learn a contemplative mode of being, an open, unencumbered heart that gives God the space to transform us.

This tension found in the contemplative call that Teresa describes in the fourth dwelling is summarized well in these words of Thomas Merton:

> It is not enough to remain the same "self," the same individual ego, with a new set of activities and a new lot of religious practices. One must be born of the Spirit who is free, and who teaches the inmost depths of the heart by taking that heart to Himself, by making Himself one with our heart, by creating for us, invisibly, a new identity: by being Himself that identity.[27]

THE THIRD DWELLING PLACES: CONCERNING THE LIFE OF A GOOD CHRISTIAN

Concerning souls that have entered the third dwelling places, . . .
the Lord has done them no small favor, but a very great one.
(The Interior Castle, III.1.5)

In the rooms of the third dwelling, the struggle becomes less intense and we find good Christians who pray on a regular basis, are dedicated to helping others, and, having avoided serious sin, are dedicated to working on the less troublesome character flaws. They have achieved a sense of security and contentment in their spiritual lives. As Teresa puts it, "Certainly, this is a state to be desired" (IC III.1.5).

For example, consider a person who is active in the community and in her church and is concerned about the welfare of others. She attends liturgy and leads a moral life. She prays on a regular basis and finds some guidance through her prayer. She assumes that she has a good relationship with God and, as often as she can, tries to be mindful of this relationship throughout the day. Her intention is to continue the behavior of a good Christian—carrying out her responsibilities and doing things that please God.

However, something within her is stirring. She lives a well-ordered and balanced life but senses an impasse on an unconscious level. Her life is an example to others, and she is a spiritual guide for some, yet even with her progress in leading a moral life and helping others, she continues to feel vulnerable to her desires, and at times finds herself on the brink of a serious fall. A path that once seemed focused and moving in one direction has faltered and has left her feeling helpless and fearful. Worse yet, her taste for spirituality has soured; her spiritual practice has become too predictable, without the wonder or surprise of revelation that she once felt. She has lost touch with her willingness to take risks and seek adventure in her relationship with God.

One of the most disturbing experiences of the impasse for her is that prayer no longer provides the same comfort that it once did. Even though she has been faithful to prayer, she now senses God's absence more than his presence.

She can't help thinking that God has deserted her. Yet she feels she deserves more, considering her progress. Should she not benefit from her years of spiritual discipline and her determination to get to this point on the spiritual path? Moreover, her dry prayer has affected the vitality of her relationships and has made her work seem mundane and difficult. The joy she once felt in being alive has disappeared, and now life itself has become more like a burdensome responsibility. She is tempted to blame her inner tension on work-related issues and the tensions in her marriage, but she knows the real problem lies elsewhere.

LACKING IN HUMILITY

I cannot help but think that anyone who makes such
an issue of this dryness is a little lacking in humility.
(*The Interior Castle*, III.1.7)

The woman above might assume that her spiritual life has broken and shattered into many irretrievable pieces. Both Teresa and John of the Cross, however, would describe her experience not as something negative but as a transitional time into a deeper relationship with divine love. Things that were once important and relied on to reinforce an image of self now fade in the dusk, losing their attraction in the brilliance of an ineffable light.

The real purpose of this darkness, according to both Teresa and John, is not to cause suffering but to dislodge the primacy of the ego—the illusory self—and, in so doing, open us to God's love. It is dark because God's action is primary; we are no longer in control and are being invited to wait and trust that divine love is working in the unconscious. As the theologian and psychiatrist Gerald May puts it, "The night is the means by which we find our heart's desire, our freedom to love."[28]

Teresa encourages us as adult Christians to continue our journey, though we may not understand it because what we perceive as an impasse is a necessary stimulus for further growth: "Enter, enter . . . into the interior rooms; pass on from your little works. By the mere fact that you are Christians you must do all these things and much more" (IC III.1.6).

Because it will always entail a growing openness to God's mysterious ways in our lives, the entire spiritual journey, we might assume, will be an ongoing relationship with darkness. Gerald May suggests that "the dark night of the soul is not an event one passes through and gets beyond, but rather a deep ongoing process that characterizes our spiritual life."[29]

Instead of trusting the darkness, some will retreat to their former spiritual practices, which at one time made them feel successful and able to grow. They feel put out by the suffering and complain about the absence of reinforcement. Teresa sees this reaction as a lack of humility. This rough path, she counsels, is an invitation to the next step in growth. God is setting us up, so to speak, so that "out of dryness you may draw humility—and not disquiet"(IC III.1.9). If we insist on continuing to retreat to our former ways, even though these once provided an enriching experience, we demonstrate an unwillingness to hand our lives over to God. In following our own will, we cause our own suffering.

John of the Cross adds to Teresa's description. He refers to "beginners" at this stage who, because they are "aware of their own imperfections, grow angry with the themselves in an unhumble impatience. . . . They want to become saints in a day."[30] Beginners depend on their own resources, says John, and they make plenty of resolutions, breaking many of them, causing themselves even more frustration and anger. They lack the patience to wait for what God is offering in his own time. Most of all, a beginner fails to see that no matter how much attention and effort he gives to relinquishing the self, he "will never be able to do so entirely—far from it—until God accomplishes it in him passively by means of the purgation of this night."[31]

The question is simple: do we want to forge ahead in our well-ordered, well-disciplined, and secure lives even though we have a nagging sense, highlighted by an inner disquiet and lack of passion, that something is missing?

In the rooms of this third dwelling, we come to a critical point in our journey in which we have found some temporary solace and success in our spirituality, but it is clear that this is not enough. Are we willing to put ourselves to the test and answer a more radical call of love? Teresa is quick to remind us that the impetus for the journey from the beginning was not our will but God's, and without God nothing is possible. We are being called to relinquish our own efforts to plan and control our lives and take a stance of receptivity and openness: a movement from prayer in the thinking, discursive manner to a simplified awareness of God's presence.

WHAT MORE DO I NEED TO DO?

From the time I began to speak of these dwelling places I have had this young man in mind. For we are literally like him.
(The Interior Castle, III.1.6)

Teresa understood that the best approach to the spiritual challenge that occurs in the rooms of the third dwelling can be found in the Gospel of Matthew, the story of the rich young man who seeks guidance from Christ.

> And now a man came to him and asked, "Master, what good deed must I do to possess eternal life?" Jesus said to him, "Why do you ask me about what is good? There is one alone who is good. But if you wish to enter into life, keep the commandments." . . . The young man said to him, "I have kept all these. What more do I need to do?" Jesus said, "If you wish to be perfect, go and sell your possessions and give the money to the poor, and you will have treasure in heaven; then come, follow me." But when the young man heard these words he went away sad, for he was a man of great wealth. (Matthew 19:16-17, 20-22)

In order to identify with the passage, take a moment to put yourself into the scene. You are the rich young man who, on a path outside of town, sees Jesus approaching you from the opposite direction. You realize that you cannot be satisfied with a greeting but that you have a deep need to speak with Jesus. Get in touch with your heart. What is welling up within you? What is drawing you toward Jesus?

As you approach Jesus, your heart spills over and the rawness and immediacy of your question surprise you. Listen to your words. "What more do I need to do?" you ask. You have kept the commandments, behaved well, and feel good about your success, and now you sense that this is not enough, that something is missing.

Jesus responds, "If you wish to be perfect, go and sell your possessions and give the money to the poor, and you will have treasure in heaven; then come, follow me." You are startled by

Jesus' words, and as they sink in, you realize that he is asking you to give up your very life, your identity, the way that others are accustomed to seeing you.

You recognize with a flash of intuition that what Jesus offers is the happiness you seek. However, you find yourself turning away to leave, heavyhearted and alone. The full weight of the life you have built rests heavily on your shoulders. All of the security, pleasure, and comfort, all that you have identified with as uniquely you, pull you downward. Yet you are not ready to let go.

You did not think that Jesus would ask you for such a complete surrender of your will. You approached him with enthusiasm and hope, and now you leave disheartened. You are a good person who has tried to live a good life; you have done what the Church has asked of you; you pray and have been diligent in practicing your religion. Why is this not enough? Why did Jesus put you on the spot? You did nothing wrong! What does he want from you?

Teresa makes this point: you may be satisfied with your life, but is that enough? Are you willing, for the sake of love, to sacrifice your very will? If you are not ready in humility to surrender your whole self, then how can you expect to truly follow Christ? Have you not discovered that "doing our own will is usually what harms us" (IC III.2.12)? The young man is being asked to join his will with the will of Christ. Teresa asks each of us, "What are you being called to do in order to continue the journey?"

Love is at issue here. The surrender to love is the "perfection" that Jesus calls us to and which Teresa stresses throughout the journey. Love, Teresa reminds us, is not fabricated by the imagination or perpetuated by a haze of good feelings but shows itself in action: "For perfection . . . does not consist in spiritual delights but in greater love and in deeds done with greater justice and truth" (IC III.2.10). We are called to respond with wholehearted gratitude to a compassionate and generous God who has given us so much.

LET LOVE OVERWHELM REASON

Love has not yet reached the point of overwhelming reason.
(The Interior Castle, III.2.7)

Teresa warns us that we can easily get stuck in the rooms of this third dwelling if we hold on to what is reasonable—namely, the spiritual attitude and practices we have taken care to cultivate over the years. Reason tells us to renew our spiritual life by becoming more diligent, putting forth more effort. Certainly grace is important, but are we not the ones in charge, and have we not had success in the past?

The reality is that we are so focused on putting our unique stamp on the journey that there is no room for God. Teresa summarizes this condition succinctly: "With humility present, this stage is a most excellent one. If humility is lacking, we will remain here our whole life—and with a thousand afflictions and miseries" (IC III.2.9). Humility teaches forgetfulness of self and abandonment to divine love; it releases the heart from the burden of making the self a project, a focal point, and uncovers a deeper passion for a true self, one that is rooted in love.

This forgetfulness of self goes counter to our cultural tendencies today. Rather than having a willingness to hand over our lives in prayer or in relationships, we tend to take control, pursue an ambition, work toward the next rung of success. We are driven to prove that our lives have value and meaning. Our culture is individualistic, prizing independence above all else. This rational, controlling approach is symbolized in the products that are manufactured and sold with such popularity, such as computers, cell phones, or any number of technological devices that help us regulate and dictate our routines. Often such devices ensure that we feel rushed even when we have little to do. Sports and entertainment, among other events, are manipulated to give the appearance of being valuable and necessary for our welfare.

No wonder we tend to dig in when it comes to the spiritual life, to reinforce the same disciplines that have worked in the past, to dutifully forge ahead in our prayer, ritual, and generosity toward others. We think that progress depends on our efforts, our attempts to change our behavior in order to become better Christians. We want to please God, and we hope to resurrect the feelings that once reinforced our efforts. Without much reflection, we assume that salvation depends on how hard we work, when in reality, even during each moment of each day, we can only be saved by God's grace and unconditional love.

The theologian and psychiatrist Gerald May contends that today we are particularly susceptible to a "happiness mentality," which entails using "prayer, meditation, and worship as ways of bolstering self-importance."[32] This mentality presumes that, through our work, we can become holy, and being holy will make us happy. Prayer, then, is used as a means to alleviate suffering or bring about good feelings of peace or joy. We pray with the expectation of some payoff, and when it does not occur, we question whether our prayer was heard or not. Times of dryness bring great frustration because we assume that we are in control, and therefore we must be doing something wrong.

Teresa suggests that fear prevents love from overwhelming reason. We have good intentions and do the right thing, but this fear will not go away. It continues to haunt us. What more is being asked? If changing behavior is not enough, then what else? Is love asking for more than I can give? Am I truly called to place myself completely in the hands of God and simply trust in this loving presence without doing anything?

Let Us Abandon Our Reason and Our Fears

Let us exert ourselves . . . for the love of the Lord;
let's abandon our reason and our fears into His hands; let's forget
this natural weakness. (The Interior Castle, III.2.8)

The primary concern for Teresa is not what we do but what God has done for us through Christ and continues to work in us through the presence of the Holy Spirit. God gazes upon us lovingly, she reminds us. Now is the time to let go of our reasonable and controlled approach to life and surrender more completely to this love, which does not demand that we be worthy of it. She invites us, both religious and laypeople, to release our cherished mask of a "good person" and hand ourselves over completely to the creative action of the Spirit.

This is an invitation to a contemplative stance, one that involves less and less emphasis on our activity and control and more and more on simply being with God, living in God's presence, and allowing the Spirit of God to sustain and guide us.

Of course, such a radical transformation will be both unnerving and painful because it means displacing the ego that we have cultivated from early on. Though ego development is necessary, it eventually has to give way to a deeper authentic self, the self in Christ. However, this is not our work, but the work of the Spirit in which we participate. We are being called to a new freedom in love. Certainly we have experienced a degree of freedom up to this point, but now we are invited to an even greater freedom, one that creates space for the gifts of the Spirit and releases a hunger for true intimacy with God.

It should be emphasized that to live contemplatively—that is, to remain open to the inbreaking of the Spirit—means cultivating particular spiritual disciplines, such as taking time for prayer, reflection, and leisure. Teresa herself recommends all of this, even at the beginning of our journey. However, the hardest thing for us is to relax our egos enough so that we can get in touch with the rhythm of love being poured out by the Holy Spirit into our daily lives and allow this rhythm to be our guide. Teresa calls us to cultivate this open, spacious consciousness so that we can more easily recognize the movement of the Spirit in our everyday experience.

A GENTLE DRAWING INWARD

But one noticeably senses a gentle drawing inward. . . . It seems to me I have read where it was compared to . . . a turtle drawing into its shell. (The Interior Castle, IV.3.3)

In describing the rooms of the third dwelling, Teresa suggests that we may at some point experience recollection that is less active and does not involve much of our effort and that rises within us unexpectedly and becomes an invitation to contemplation. The purpose of this passive recollection is "to invite souls by the sight of what takes place in the remaining dwelling places . . . so that they will prepare themselves to enter them" (IC III.2.9). In other words, we receive a taste, a kind of preview, to what the remaining dwellings have to offer. Perhaps that will help us release our grip on our former life and more readily commit to the journey ahead.

Teresa thoroughly appreciates that not everyone will receive the grace of contemplative prayer, but she writes with the intention of affirming those who are invited and helping them recognize and embrace their call. Her guidance, I suspect, speaks loudly and clearly to many today who find themselves drawn to the contemplative dimension of their lives but are confused about the transition from a prayer that depends mostly on their own effort and one that is primarily God's work.

In describing this movement into a passive form of recollection, Teresa refers to Christ at the center of the castle who, like a good shepherd, calls out with a whistle so gentle that it could easily go unnoticed. Though soft as a whisper, the whistle has such power over the listeners, says Teresa, "that they abandon the exterior things . . . and enter the castle" (IC IV.3.2). This call evokes a deep receptivity in us, a contemplative posture of listening that allows God to continue to transform us.

The nineteenth-century theologian and philosopher Soren Kierkegaard offers us this personal glimpse into the discovery of a more receptive form of prayer:

And what happened then, if you did indeed pray with real inwardness? Something wonderful. For as you prayed more and more inwardly, you had less and less to say, and finally you became entirely silent. . . . You became a listener. You had thought that praying was about speaking: you learned that praying is not merely keeping silent but is listening. . . . Praying is not listening to oneself speak but is about becoming silent and, in becoming silent, waiting, until the one who prays hears God. . . . Begin praying—but not as if prayer always began with silence . . . but because when prayer really has become prayer, it becomes silence.[33]

In another analogy, making the same point, Teresa says that we respond to God's call like a turtle pulling inward, withdrawing into its shell (IC IV.3.3). This gentle movement inward is not a process we control; it is solely a matter of grace. It is not a passing feeling but leads to a serious commitment to solitude and silence and the ongoing nurturing of the inner life. Whereas our attention was once primarily turned outward, it is now drawn within us. Everything changes because now we are invited to let go of our effort to generate an experience and simply hand ourselves over. We are asked to wait like a beggar, hands outstretched, trusting that God will provide all we need.

We still meditate, says Teresa, but realize that there is no need to resort to anything other than the desire to simply remain in God's presence like a child in the arms of a parent. Prayer becomes less a formal discipline and more a response to the inbreaking of the Spirit. It is a time of watching and waiting with an appreciation of our dependence on God, not a time for thinking and activity. Any show of force will cause this inner rhythm of watching and waiting to weaken. Rather, we must learn to appreciate the importance of protecting our solitude. As Teresa advises, "Leave the soul in God's hands, let Him do whatever He wants with it, with the . . . greatest resignation to the will of God" (IC IV.3.6).

According to Teresa, the best way to nourish this inner movement or passive recollection is to stay out of the way. Even though this receptive form of recollection feels foreign because it goes contrary to our usual active recollection that we have cultivated through meditation, she advises that we give the Spirit room to work. We need to trust that God works in hidden ways to create space in our hearts and expand the soul, thus removing obstacles and introducing us to a greater freedom to love.

We also nurture this more passive recollection by letting go of the parade of thoughts and feelings that flows through our consciousness. According to Teresa, "Without any effort or noise the soul should strive to cut down the rambling of the intellect. . . . ; it is good to be aware that one is in God's presence and of who God is" (IC IV.3.7).

As we have mentioned before, simple loving awareness is enough. It is important not to think much but to love much. Release your heart so that it can long for God and enjoy this mysterious presence.

If this taste of contemplative prayer leads to a sense of being absorbed in God for a brief time, then fine; if not, return to your meditation, Teresa advises. But it is important not to try to understand what is happening because the experience of being drawn inward is sheer gift. Just enjoy the movement and keep alive a simple prayer of longing with a few loving words. Without putting up any resistance, let the grace of these rooms find a home within you.

The Fourth Dwelling Places:
Water Rises from This Spring

*It seems that since that heavenly water begins to rise from this
spring I'm mentioning that is deep within us, it swells and
expands our whole interior being, producing ineffable blessings.
(The Interior Castle, IV.2.6)*

Teresa loves the image of water so much that she admits,
"I don't find anything more appropriate to explain some
spiritual experiences than water" (IC IV.2.2). The sound of
waves rhythmically hitting the shoreline, the sight of an endless ocean horizon, or the splashing and gurgling of a forest
stream as it meanders through a dense canopy of trees—all
of these may have transfixed us at some time, and so we can
identify with her passion.

Water has an archetypal hold on the imagination. As
Christians, we are immersed in water at baptism, symbolizing
our passage through death into life. For Teresa, the symbol of
water inspired a way of describing the journey into the depths
of human consciousness to find union with God. Her yearning
for the water of eternal life echoes the emphasis in the Gospel
of John. John favors the image of a spring bubbling forth water,
the source of life itself, enlivening us and the world.

Picture a hillside spring welling up with fresh water and spill-
ing out into a lush garden landscape. Jesus cries out, "Let anyone
who is thirsty come to me!" (John 7:37). Teresa especially loved
the story of the Samaritan woman at the well because it represented her deep thirst for divine love from the time she was a

child when "I often begged the Lord to give me the water" (BL 30.19). She even carried a picture of the event with her.

In describing the "prayer of quiet," which, for Teresa, is contemplation in the strict sense—prayer that is beyond personal effort and simply gift—she draws on the image of a fountain that can be filled with water in two ways. On one hand, the water is brought in from a great distance by aqueducts or some other means, demanding a great deal of human effort. In the second way, the water rises up from beneath the fountain by a fertile spring that overflows the fountain and spills out into a large stream. The water that demands labor refers to meditative prayer; the latter, rushing up from the depths and pouring out spontaneously, refers to the prayer of quiet (IC IV.2-3).

What more can be said of the prayer of quiet? It is intimacy with the divine, the experience of an inner spring of love, abundant and overflowing, that brings great joy. "This prayer, then, is a little spark of the Lord's true love which He begins to enkindle in the soul; and He desires that the soul grow in the understanding of what this love accompanied by delight is" (BL 15.4). The joy of this prayer is beyond description: a person realizes that God is very near, although, according to Teresa, the experience does not last for very long. The spring rises up and fills the inner core of the self, and for the first time the person appreciates what it means to be happy. Our former sense of happiness and everything we imagined it to be now seems secondary.

The result of all this is a greater awareness of inner stillness and deep peace. God "produces this delight with the greatest peace and quiet and sweetness in the very interior part of ourselves" (IC IV.2.4). Teresa contrasts the consolations or joy of prayer, which depends mostly on our activity, with spiritual delight, the inner peace and sweetness of the prayer of quiet. The former can be related to the natural high we receive from extending ourselves to those in need; the latter is radically different because it originates in God, enlarges the spirit, and flows from the inner self outward.

The quiet of this infused prayer refers not to an external quiet but to a deep sense of stillness and tranquility within us. God captivates the will with love, and the memory and mind stop racing in every direction and become attentive to one thing. If the intellect and memory stray, then the will, united with God, brings them back. We do not control the prayer; it lasts as long as God wants. In Teresa's experience, it could last for a short time or for a few days; when it did last longer, her will was firmly fixed on God as she went about her daily routine. Her union with God in the prayer of quiet allowed her to be truly a contemplative in action.

How do we determine whether we are experiencing an authentic prayer of quiet or whether our inner quiet is simply the result of deep relaxation? Teresa tells us that the latter "produces no effect, quickly goes away, and leaves behind aridity" (BL 15.9). It is no surprise, then, that those who try to produce inner quiet find that it quickly dissipates as time progresses and, rather than nourishing our spirit, seems to leave it without resources.

Teresa advises that even in arid prayer, when the mind roams and the imagination goes wild, the Spirit works without our knowledge, increasing love. The desert experience, then, should not be resisted but embraced. We should remain still, return to God at the center of our beings as often as we need to, and not give in to feelings of depression or, worst of all, stop praying. We could also choose to return to meditation, which she believed was truly effective for growth even at this stage of prayer.

Because the joy and peace of the prayer of quiet are so pleasurable, it is easy to become attached and try to rekindle it. To do so is to forget that the prayer is a gift we do not deserve. Our ongoing response should be one of gratitude. "Almost everything lies in finding oneself unworthy of so great a good and in being occupied with giving thanks" (IC IV.3.8). Any effort on our part will only bring on dryness and increasing restlessness; in other words, our interference would be like "throwing water on [the flame] and killing it" (BL 15.4). Never forget, Teresa reminds us, that the source of our joy is God, not our own ability to quiet ourselves.

THIS TURMOIL OF MIND

I have been very afflicted at times in the midst of this turmoil of mind. . . . Ordinarily the mind flies about quickly.
(The Interior Castle, IV.1.8)

In her poem "Flickering Mind," Denise Levertov describes the difficulty of keeping the mind still even for a second. Expressing the concern of anyone who prays, she wonders how she can focus long enough to see "at the fountain's heart / the sapphire I know is there."[34]

Teresa strained against her own unruly mind and found it difficult to understand its workings. She questioned the hold that distractions had on her and their intensity, particularly when she was centered in God's presence: "I have seen, I think, that the faculties of my soul were occupied and recollected in God while my mind on the other hand was distracted. This distraction puzzled me" (IC IV.1.8). She was puzzled because she expected that distractions would stop once her will was captivated by divine love, not realizing that in the initial stages of contemplation, the memory and understanding had remained unfettered.

Teresa's candor is refreshing because we, too, identify with the tenacity of distractions: the tug of thoughts in every direction, seductive desires and worldly concerns, unexpected feelings that stream through our consciousness, preventing us from being present to God. If we give in to one of them, it sets off an avalanche that cannot be controlled. However, it helps to remember that even Jesus was attacked by demons during his forty-day retreat in the wilderness (Mark 1:12-13).

Teresa found that growth in prayer necessarily means dealing with distractions that try to pull us away from our single-minded pursuit of God. The closer she came to the center of the castle, the more she found her mind entertaining the noise and attachments outside its walls.

According to Teresa, some distractions arise from a disordered will. They are messengers from the ego that we have cultivated for most of our lives. Because we lack self-knowledge, we have to engage in an inner struggle in which we hear noise and deal with confusion that we have created through all our attachments. Teresa writes that "for the most part all the trials and disturbances come from our not understanding ourselves" (IC IV.1.9). She advises that we keep our conscience pure because anything that binds the heart will become an issue during prayer. Rather than concentrating on stopping distractions, we should put our energy into practicing the virtues of love, detachment, and humility.

As prayer deepens and self-knowledge grows, we discover the true self in Christ. This awareness, however, only intensifies the struggle with distractions because the illusory self, which we have cultivated for a good part of our lives, recognizes the seriousness of the threat. Now distractions rise up like soldiers in rebellion intent on stopping any further advance inward. The person recognizes that the ego must be sacrificed but finds herself in a battle.

Once we are aware of distractions as the offspring of the illusory self's need to be in control, we can keep watch over our thoughts and realize which ones provoke us. Perhaps it is anger, fear, or pride. Instead of following a thought and developing a commentary, we simply let go and then return to our loving attentiveness to the call within us: "One should leave the intellect go and surrender oneself into the arms of love" (IC IV.3.8). We release thoughts as they sail by on the current of consciousness and return repeatedly to the depths of the heart to listen.

There are also other kinds of distractions, according to Teresa—those that are not due to our self-centeredness but, like flies on a windowsill buzzing about with no real target, simply cause noise and confusion. How should we respond? "Whoever experiences the affliction these distractions cause will see that they are not his fault; he should not grow anxious, which makes things worse, or tire himself trying to put order into something that at the time doesn't have any. . . . He should pray as best he can; or even not pray . . . ; let him occupy himself in other works of virtue" (WP 24.5). In a very practical way, she advises that if the distractions are too much, then turn your attention to a practice that refreshes the soul; don't try to force your prayer.

Even though Teresa was truly bothered by her restless mind and tried hard to bring it under control, she soon concluded that ultimately, it is out of our hands and there is no point in being disturbed. Just "let the millclapper go clacking on" (IC IV.1.13).

However, Teresa warns us not to take distractions lightly, and above all, do not let them prevent us from praying. So how do we handle them when they arise? Begin by recognizing and naming them when they appear. This becomes easier the more you pray. Then dismiss them immediately before they can detour your attention. Remember that a loving relationship is the point, not a prayer technique or your success with distractions, "so do that which best stirs you to love" (IC IV.1.7).

To spark this love, Teresa advocates using simple words to guide the heart back to its center again and again. John of the Cross reassures us that "the soul lives where she loves . . . and lives through love in the object of her love."[35] We join Teresa in her prayer: "Lord, bring us to the place where these miseries will not taunt us" (IC IV.1.12).

At certain times during prayer, distractions may cease altogether. (In fact, a person may pass in and out of the various experiences during a single period of prayer.) When this happens, the powers of the soul are immersed in God, asleep in the divine, so that we are not aware of ourselves praying. The troubles with the wandering mind cease, at least for the time that the experience lasts. Because the Spirit's work within us remains hidden from our consciousness, we recognize what has happened only afterwards. Teresa assures us that though the experience may last only a short time and may remain shrouded in mystery, it transforms us in unexplainable ways, and the good effects of the prayer influences all our actions.

Suggestions for Reflection

1. Do you find yourself secure and comfortable in the practice of your faith? Are you experiencing any deep stirrings that seem to be asking something more from you? If so, describe this awareness of being unsettled and how you have responded.

2. How does the story of the rich young man in Matthew 19:16-22 mirror your own call to follow Jesus? How have you responded to Jesus' invitation to release all attachments and open yourself to the image of Christ within you?

3. Can you identify with Teresa's lack of interest in discursive prayer or for using the imagination? Teresa often used a book or the beauty of nature to focus her attention and prevent her mind from roaming. What do you do to keep your attention focused during prayer?

4. In your own experience of the spiritual life, and prayer in particular, how have you allowed love to overwhelm reason?

5. Have you experienced a call to a more simplified awareness of God and a greater self-forgetfulness? If so, how have you responded? Have you integrated silent prayer into your spiritual practice? What was the effect of this experience on you over time?

6. What guidance from Teresa has spoken to your heart? How can you integrate this wisdom into your life?

Chapter Five

Longing for Union

True union can very well be reached, with God's help,
if we make the effort to obtain it by keeping our wills fixed
only on that which is God's will.
—*The Interior Castle, V.3.3*

Having journeyed beyond the secure rooms of the third dwelling and taken a risk for the sake of love, those who enter the rooms of the remaining dwellings now know the pleasure, joy, and freedom of a deeper relationship with God.

They have tasted the joy of a simplified prayer and experienced the inner peace of contemplation, the prayer of quiet, but continue to feel incomplete. They are not yet at home and long for a greater union. The prayer of quiet has opened the door to the rooms of the three remaining dwellings closer to the center of the castle. The journey continues.

The Fifth Dwelling Places: This Union Is above All Earthly Joys

This union is above all earthly joys, above all delights, above all consolations. . . . The difference is like that between feeling something on the rough outer covering of the body or in the marrow of the bones.
(The Interior Castle, V.1.6)

Are we at least safe, at this stage, from falling backwards into the rooms of former dwellings?

Teresa warns, as she has previously, that the forces of evil and our own destructive behavior can still undermine our growth unless we take care. Humility has been the guiding light all along, and now it is even more essential. We may feel confident in our path because the usual temptations no longer seem to control our behavior, but spiritual pride lurks in the shadows and can undermine the gifts we have received. We should ask ourselves repeatedly one critical question: "Have I lost touch with humility by being satisfied with my progress and becoming proud of the grace I have received?"

Also, at this point in the journey the temptation is to assume that entrance into the remaining dwellings is restricted to saints like Teresa. After all, it is difficult to imagine that the mystical states that Teresa describes can be related to everyday activities such as grocery shopping, preparing the family meal, or spending time with friends. Are we simply out of our depth and no longer able to identify with Teresa, along with other saints and mystics who have received such special graces?

Teresa would disagree. She encourages us to look forward to the journey ahead. We may not experience her heightened state nor live fully in all the dwellings, but with grace we can have a brief glimpse of what is to come. We can also appreciate the importance of the dwellings as inspiration for further growth.

Most important, according to Teresa, is that maturation in prayer does not remove us from this world but anchors us in it more authentically, with even greater compassion and willingness to serve others. While her own experiences of ecstasy are unique, she emphasizes that such extraordinary experiences are not essential for growth in prayer. As a matter of fact, they can become handicaps, drawing attention to themselves and away from what is really important.

Teresa believed that the rooms of the fifth dwelling were accessible to most of her nuns but that only a few would experience all the rooms that she had. She was also quick to admit that if she could, she would remain silent about what is found in these rooms because they are shrouded in mystery, beyond the reach of intellect or imagination. She makes her position clear: "I believe it would be better not to say anything about these remaining rooms, for there is no way of knowing how to speak of them" (IC V.1.1).

What is important for Teresa, as always, is not the stage in which we find ourselves but our continued willingness to surrender. It is not the pleasure we discover in prayer as we grow, but our desire to identify with the will of God more completely and undergo a transformation that purifies and illuminates the depths of our being on every level. Prayer, then, becomes a way of life, a continuing process of this transformation toward eventual union that both Teresa and John of the Cross refer to as "spiritual marriage."

A painting by Vincent van Gogh, *The Prison Courtyard*, highlights the great difference between the beginning of our pilgrimage outside the walls of the castle and our present state in the rooms of this fifth dwelling. In the painting, prisoners are taking their exercise in a small courtyard, walking in a tight circle surrounded by towering stone walls. Shoulders hunched and heads down, they trudge past the guards. They are reminders of the lack of freedom and the depression we once experienced outside the castle walls when we felt restricted and had little awareness of what was important. In contrast, high above the prisoners, two white butterflies fly about freely in the vibrant air, symbolizing the freedom that awaits those who move through the dwellings toward the center of the castle.

Like van Gogh, Teresa chose the little white butterfly to represent the promise of paradise and pure freedom.

A LITTLE WHITE BUTTERFLY

Oh, now, to see the restlessness of this little butterfly,
even though it has never been quieter and calmer in its life.
(The Interior Castle, V.2.8)

My wife plants butterfly bushes and other brightly colored flowers around the yard for the sole purpose of attracting butterflies. It is mesmerizing, on butterfly days, to see these airy visitors float into the garden, blown in by a soft breeze. Butterflies settle on a blossom and raise their multicolored wings in an arch; then, another breeze, and they are gone.

Teresa was drawn to the image of butterflies and, in particular, to their process of metamorphosis. Carmelite author Fr. John Welch highlights Teresa's use of butterfly symbols and suggests that the transformation of a silkworm to cocoon to butterfly can summarize the soul's entire pilgrimage through the castle. He points out that although Teresa mistook moths for butterflies, having heard of this transformative process through hearsay, her description of the butterfly's development still works as a symbol of the inner journey.[36]

At the beginning of the pilgrimage, in the rooms of dwellings one through three, we pursue self-knowledge, particularly with the help of vocal prayers and meditation and the practice of virtue. We fan the inner flame of love with Scripture, the beauty of nature, and books on spirituality. We cultivate a receptivity to grace, opening our hearts to receive the gifts that God offers. Like caterpillars, we possess a ravenous appetite to know ourselves in a deeper spiritual way.

Then the journey takes an abrupt turn. The first three stages do not lead to a peaceful plateau but rather to an impasse. We realize that our lives are not in our control but must now be surrendered to God's action in us. In preparation, we create space within ourselves through detachment, renouncing self-love and self-will. For the silkworm, the cocoon is "the house wherein it will die" (IC V.2.4). Like the silkworm, the cocoon we spin represents our life hidden in Christ. As Paul declares, "You have died, and now the life you have is hidden with Christ in God" (Colossians 3:3). Teresa presses us to keep in mind the urgency of our participation in the Spirit's work: "Let's be quick to do this work and weave this little cocoon by getting rid of our self-love and self-will, our attachment to any earthly thing"(IC V.2.6).

The transformation occurs in the rooms of the fifth dwelling. The fertile darkness of the cocoon represents our relationship with a mysterious God and the promise of a new birth of intimacy: "When the soul is, in this prayer [of union], truly dead to the world, a little white butterfly comes forth" (IC V.2.7). This transformation is all God's work, Teresa assures us. The soul, coming out of this prayer, no longer recognizes itself. How different it is from the person it was before, like the difference between a tiny silkworm and a butterfly. Union with God is experienced as profound freedom; the butterfly emerges in all its grandeur and beauty.

THE UNION I DESIRED ALL MY LIFE

This union with God's will is the union I have desired
all my life; it is the union I ask the Lord for always.
(The Interior Castle, V.3.5)

This transformation, as we have seen, is not limited to the rooms of a particular dwelling but is an ongoing life journey. It began in the rooms of the fourth dwelling and will continue until the end, the seventh. Why? Because, as Teresa puts it, the little butterfly is restless, and even though it now experiences deep peace and freedom, it can only be fulfilled by complete union with God.

Restlessness drives us because we realize that the things of this earth will never feed our hunger; the world wearies us because we realize it cannot offer deep peace. Teresa asks how we can remain satisfied with walking when we have learned how to fly. Once experienced, the joy and freedom of this new life help the pilgrim, who is now even more aware of the pain of separation from God, to continue to die to self with the promise of new life.

Following Teresa's example, we can see our own story as one of ongoing transformation that will involve dying and rising. Restlessness is the cross that we bear as pilgrims on earth, but for Teresa, it is a necessary one. There is no need to be despondent, however, since there is peace in knowing that "God wants [us] to be living in this exile" (IC V.2.10). The journey of prayer continues because even though union has been tasted, the pilgrim has yet to come to the center of the castle; she is "not entirely surrendered to God's will" (V.2.10).

This Prayer of Union

When the soul is, in this prayer, truly dead to the world,
a little white butterfly comes forth. Oh, greatness of God!
(The Interior Castle, V.2.7)

Teresa emphasizes that the prayer of union, which is the signature experience of the fifth dwelling, is pure gift; no method or technique will produce it. Also, the person in this state, which she says lasts for a short period of time, will not be aware of the union.

However, Teresa assures us that this union transcends any human experience and evades description: "Don't think this union is some kind of dreamy state. . . . As a matter of fact, during the time that the union lasts the soul is left as though without its senses, for it has no power to think even if it wants to. . . . In sum, it is like one who in every respect has died to the world so as to live more completely in God" (IC V.1.4).

Though the prayer of union is deeper than the prayer of quiet, it is still not complete. In the prayer of quiet, we participate in grace but receive no help that is out of the ordinary, explains Teresa. In the prayer of union, however, the soul is drawn toward the center by divine action: God communicates with it directly while all human powers—memory, will, and understanding—remain captivated, unable to be a distraction. In the past, only the will was asleep.

Teresa, drawing on the rich tradition of bridal mysticism, describes the prayer of union as occurring before betrothal. This encounter with Christ before betrothal is a chance to explore the relationship and find common ground. In the period of betrothal, the knowledge of another grows into love, and then, in marriage, there is complete surrender to each other. These stages reflect Spanish custom in sixteenth-century Spain, but Teresa is using them as a symbol of a purely spiritual love.

At this point, there is no longer a need to put forth the effort demanded in meditation or discursive prayer. The soul simply lets God do the work; it is purely receptive, like wax in God's hands: "The wax doesn't impress the seal upon itself; it is only disposed—I mean by being soft" (IC V.2.12). Teresa adds that we do not soften ourselves but simply remain still, quiet, and open, offering no hindrance to God's work. Drawing on the search for the Beloved in the Song of Songs, Teresa says that our search will lead to "the wine cellar where the Lord wishes to place us when He desires and as He desires. But however great the effort we make to do so, we cannot enter. . . . He doesn't want our will to have any part to play, for it has been entirely surrendered to Him" (V.1.12). The beautiful and seductive image of an inner wine cellar describes a new order of love, a deep centering, and an inner peace.

Because this union, then, is beyond joy, pleasure, and all experience in a way that "the soul doesn't recognize itself" (IC V.2.7), it remains indescribable. How do you know that your time was spent in communion with God? Because when the soul becomes aware of itself once again, "it can in no way doubt that it was in God and God was in it" (V.1.9). In fact, if we are aware of ourself during prayer, then separation between self and God remains, and union was not complete. The highest form of prayer is when the person praying is not aware of the prayer.

The difference between the life before and the life after this prayer of union is like the difference between the tiny silkworm and its metamorphosis into the little white butterfly. However, as Teresa reminds us, the deep peace and delight of this prayer do not remove the suffering and trials that afflicted the person before the experience. She learned this lesson firsthand.

Even as she was writing *The Interior Castle* in 1582, Teresa experienced betrayal, backbiting, and persecutions, all of which threatened her life's work. She fought through this difficult period with determination and was even able to see it with a certain lighthearted objectivity. Her trials would continue even after these persecutions had ended. In addition to her already poor health, she became so ill from a bout with influenza that she almost died, and the boundless energy that had fueled her vocation for so many years was beginning to be drained by the inevitable infirmities of aging. Through all of these setbacks, she insisted on continuing in God's service.

In the end, the real test of our inner growth, insists Teresa, is not some extraordinary spiritual experience but love of neighbor. If you want to know where you stand in your prayer life, even though there are significant signs that you love God, look to the love you express toward others. Teresa assures us that "the more advanced you see you are in love for your neighbor the more advanced you will be in the love of God" (IC V.3.8). There are those who have visions and extraordinary experiences yet are not close to God, and there are others whose prayer seems ordinary, but because they are faithful to what God desires for them in service to others, they are near to him.

THE SIXTH DWELLING PLACES:
TRIALS AND GRACES

For truly, when one is suffering the trials,
it then seems that everything is lost.
(The Interior Castle, VI.1.3)

As we have seen in the prayer of union, the butterfly emerges and there is new life. However, Teresa cautions us not to assume that at this stage of the path, having received favors from God, we no longer have temptation and attachments from the past to deal with or that we "have nothing to fear nor sins to weep over" (IC VI.7.1). The temptation to sin may be less intense, but the struggle will continue. Most of all, it is hard to forget, even at this point, how ungrateful we are for the love we have received.

The soul is not yet completely free; the pilgrimage continues. In the rooms of the sixth dwelling, Teresa describes the process of purification, which is comparable to the dark night of faith associated with St. John of the Cross. There is a sense of abandonment; the inner life feels like a desert, and faith and virtues seem to disappear. No relief from the suffering can be found, either from within us or outside of us.

A painful dimension of this night is the loss of our familiar relationship with God. The theologian and psychiatrist Gerald May explains that "the word 'God' loses its meaning. That word, which used to bring forth familiar images and feelings, now seems inadequate and somehow even wrong. And there seems to be no satisfactory substitute."[37] The seeker, then, must affirm the darkness, realizing that no name can describe the ultimate reality of God. To hold on to our feelings and images of God, particularly at this stage, gives them more significance than the reality to which they point.

Perhaps even more disturbing is that we lose a sense of God's presence, which has been so nourishing in the past. We have been accustomed to sensing God's presence through relationships, in nature, or in special places, and these experiences have fed our soul. Now these experiences dry up, and it feels as if God has forgotten us. Some time later, we recognize that this change is an invitation to let go of our attachment to feelings and images that surround our relationship with God and to accept God as God.

Teresa experienced this dark night of the soul as a loss of meaning and hope, as if one is set adrift on an ocean without the possibility of moorings. She started to doubt her journey and the authenticity of the divine love that she had experienced. Was it an illusion? Was she also deceived about her progress? Is the journey a sham and her good works only a projection of her neediness?

Teresa also found herself without support. Confessors questioned her experience, linking it to demonic temptation or depression. Social approval also turned against her; she was relegated to the fringe of the community and criticized for her extraordinary experiences. However, even the praise that she received made her suffer, since she desired with her whole being that this praise be directed to God, not to herself. Physical pain and illness were ongoing, as they had been for most of her life. There was no way out of the darkness. Her only response was a plea: "Oh, God help me! Lord, how You afflict Your lovers! But everything is small in comparison with what You give them afterward" (IC VI.11.6).

How Many Times, My Lord!

How many times, my Lord, have You freed me from so dark a prison, and how often have I put myself in it again against Your will! (The Book of Her Life, 32.5).

As might be expected, even prayer gave Teresa no solace. The experience of divine intimacy itself caused her pain, since she was even more intensely aware of how much she fell short in her response to God's love. She had grown tremendously in self-knowledge and was acutely aware of a chasm between the goodness of God and her own life.

Maybe the best expression of Teresa's dark night of the spirit was her vision of hell. This revelation gave her full insight into the effects of sin. In the vision, she enters a long and narrow alley that is dark, confined, muddy, and snake-infested. At the end of the alley, she discovers a hole, which she enters. There she finds herself unable to sit or stand. She realizes that all the suffering on earth is nothing in comparison to what she finds in hell. The vision helped her realize the chasm between herself and God's love, and she was overcome by the reality and abundance of God's mercy (BL 32.1–8).

At one point during this dark night, Teresa did receive reassurance from God: she heard the words "Do not be afraid, it is I" (IC VI.8.3). These words buoyed and strengthened her spirit, assuring her that God was with her, but at the same time, they did not resolve her dilemma. She was caught between two poles—between the human and the divine—and she wanted a resolution, even if it meant death. "The soul sees that it is like a person hanging, who cannot support himself on any earthly thing; nor can it ascend to heaven. On fire with this thirst, it cannot get to the water; and the thirst is not one that is endurable but already at such a point that nothing will take it away" (VI.11.5). She yearned for death because she knew that only death would resolve this tension; nothing less than a spiritual death could heal and renew her entire being.

What is the point of all this suffering? For Teresa, the answer is simple: it is meant to intensify the longing of the heart for God. We may find it difficult to relate to her experience, but it certainly brings to light an intuition that all of us have of a growing awareness of God's love; it is both painful—because it reminds us of our true condition as human beings in need of God's mercy—and, at the same time, delightful—because the wound of love has touched the very core of our being, introducing it to the greatest happiness we have ever known.

The darkness that tests faith may remind us of a time when we, too, experienced a lack of support from others, dryness in prayer, or a sense of our distance from God. Our experience may not compare to Teresa's, but like her, we may have realized that our only option in the middle of this time of trial was "to wait for the mercy of God" (IC VI.1.10).

GOD CARRIES OFF THE ENTIRE SOUL

In a rapture, believe me, God carries off for Himself the entire soul, and, as to someone who is His own . . . , He begins showing it some little part of the kingdom that it has gained.
(The Interior Castle, VI.4.9)

To consider the rooms of the sixth dwelling only as a place of purification would be to emphasize only part of the story. Teresa also experienced many extraordinary graces. One of the most important of these—namely, rapture—penetrated to the depths of her soul and bathed it in divine bliss, causing "a new estrangement from earthly things that makes life much more arduous" (BL 20.8).

According to Teresa, rapture is an experience of contemplation that cannot be refused, as the person is swept away by love with faculties completely suspended. Afterwards, the person remembers nothing but is left with the certainty that God has taken possession of her soul.

Rapture brings with it not only indescribable love but pain at even the smallest failings because these are now exposed to God's powerful light. "The soul is like water in a glass: the water looks very clear if the sun doesn't shine on it; but when the sun shines on it, it seems to be full of dust particles" (BL 20.28). Think of walking into a room on a brilliant sunny day and seeing cobwebs in the corners, a layer of dust under some furniture, and dust particles floating in the air, all of which remain hidden on a cloudy day. The result of this revelation is true humility, says Teresa, and the heightened realization that all that is done should be done for God's glory and "that everything other than pleasing God is nothing" (21.5).

In rapture, says Teresa, the person forgets herself and her distance from God, even thinking that she is so united to God that there is no division. Rapture left Teresa with a profound awareness that she could do nothing without God, but at the same time, it gave her courage and strength to continue in God's service. Even with all its remarkable effects, the experience of rapture was also the way of the cross, causing her to see life differently, in the light of authentic truth. As a result, she possessed an extraordinary sense of freedom, and all "seems . . . to be child's play" (BL 21.9).

Teresa did not consider any of the extraordinary graces she received, like rapture, locutions, or visions, as essential. She actually saw them as a burden because of the attention they brought to her and because she knew how important it was to be responsible for discerning whether they were authentic or not.

She insisted that the importance of these experiences lies in their effect on us. Do they leave us in a state of peace and joy, or do they unsettle and depress us? Do they increase the virtues of humility and love or make us feel self-important? Teresa considered anything extraordinary to be purely a gift and nothing that she asked for or deserved. Raptures, in particular, left her with a profound realization that she could do nothing without God and that she would have to struggle with the intense loneliness of one who realizes that true happiness cannot be found in this world.

Teresa also cautions others to seek sound spiritual direction at this level of prayer. Find wise counsel, she advises, and open your heart to the instruction. She sees herself as a guide for others through her writings and prays, "Please God that I may have succeeded in explaining what I set out to; may it be helpful for whoever has had such experience" (IC VI.3.18).

Admittedly, the prayer and experiences Teresa describes in the rooms of this sixth dwelling may seem far from our own experience, but simply reading about them gives us a perspective on what it means to take seriously an intimate relationship with God. We can also identify with some of Teresa's insights because we find seeds of spiritual growth germinating within us, no matter where we are on our journey.

The journey is not over for any of us; it must continue. We are not meant to remain satisfied with any dwelling, Teresa assures us. With the support of grace and the guiding hand of humility, we continue our pilgrimage.

DEVOTION TO THE SACRED HUMANITY OF CHRIST

How much more is it necessary not to withdraw through one's own efforts from all our good and help which is the most sacred humanity of our Lord Jesus Christ.
(The Interior Castle, VI.7.6)

We might expect that in the rooms of this sixth dwelling, which concern deeply mystical prayer, Teresa would propose releasing our thoughts and images, including those on the humanity of Christ. After all, such images connect us to physical reality and therefore might hinder contemplation. Teresa certainly read authors who had mapped out a path into contemplative darkness as a way toward union with God.

However, Teresa balks at this dark path and declares that "to withdraw completely from Christ . . . , I cannot endure" (BL 22.1). She agrees that we can lose touch with the sacred humanity during contemplation, but she insists that, in general, those who abandon Christ's humanity will not enter the sixth and seventh dwellings. Only in the rooms of the seventh dwelling, she says, will meditation be unnecessary, except on rare occasions, because the person rests in the presence of divine love continually.

The strength of her dedication to the sacred humanity of Jesus originated in her own experience because she took great care to cultivate a devotion to Christ's humanity throughout her life. In meditation she focused particularly on the passion, and she favored images of Christ that reflected such titles as "good Jesus," "our Companion," "Friend," and "our Teacher." However, when she first began to enjoy the prayer of quiet, she allowed herself to believe that the humanity of Christ was an obstacle to deeper prayer. Later, she realized that this approach could be dangerous because "to be always withdrawn from corporeal things . . . is the trait of angelic spirits, not of those who live in mortal bodies" (IC VI.7.6).

She held that, no matter how advanced in prayer we are, we must not allow ourselves to think that meditation on the sacred humanity of Christ is not important. She refused to believe that we could ever reach a stage of prayer where reflecting on the Christian mysteries and Christ's passion, in particular, is no longer possible. It is precisely because we are human beings, she argues, that contemplation is not continuous; we need the intellect to spark our desire. "Life is long, and there are in it many trials, and we need to look at Christ our model" (IC VI.7.13).

Throughout the journey through the castle, she suggests a prayer of simple regard as a way of meditating, since it does not weigh down the intellect but rather keeps it open to the immediacy of Christ's presence. This method allows for the meditation, through grace, to deepen suddenly and become contemplation. The process is much like skipping a stone over the water, which, without notice, disappears into the silent depths.

For Teresa, there are two ways of approaching meditation. The first relies a great deal on the intellect and involves much reflection, relating the Christian mysteries to our lives. The second uses the mysteries as a touchstone. For example, we recall one of them, dwell on it gently, and let it spark love in our hearts. The idea is to allow the image to find a home in us. Teresa found that "the mere sight of the Lord fallen to the ground in the garden . . . is enough to last the intellect not only an hour but many days, while it looks with a simple gaze at who He is" (IC VI.7.11). This prayer of simple regard, says Teresa, always has a place in our lives, even if we experience contemplation.

There may be times when we are so filled with such love that nothing else matters, but in reality these experiences are brief. In the meantime, Teresa encourages us to use meditation and any tools available to stoke the flame within us. She cautions against remaining in a state of emptiness, in a kind of listless vacuum, in the name of contemplation.

Her emphasis is on Jesus and cultivating an intimate relationship with him from the beginning of our journey, allowing it to develop into a continual companionship. For Teresa, this did not necessitate conjuring up an image of Christ but simply being aware of his presence. Christ should not be forgotten for any reason, for "we cannot do otherwise than walk always with Him" (IC VI.8.1).

THE SEVENTH DWELLING PLACES: THE LITTLE BUTTERFLY DIES — FREEDOM

This state is the place where the little butterfly we mentioned dies, and with the greatest joy because its life is now Christ.
(The Interior Castle, VII.2.5)

The pilgrim now reaches the center of the interior castle, the goal of the journey of prayer. As Teresa describes it, this is not a state of blissful separation that removes a person from everyday reality but a deep awareness of being grounded, being whole, and being dedicated to the welfare of others. What once had seemed separate—for example, action and contemplation—are now integrated in daily life.

Christ himself brought Teresa into the rooms of the seventh mansions for the purpose of mystical marriage, or spiritual transformation. Teresa employs the symbol of a mystical marriage as a way of describing the growing intimacy between the soul and God.

Though difficult to relate to today, the mystical marriage perfectly captures the burgeoning love relationship that develops as a person passes through the rooms of the different dwellings. The symbol has it roots in salvation history. The covenant relationship in the beginning was mostly a legal relationship, but eventually it became something more personal. In time, it represented a spousal love relationship that included betrothal and marriage. The prophets, in particular, forged this new ground, beginning with Hosea: "I shall betroth you in uprightness and justice, and faithful love and tenderness" (Hosea 2:21). Isaiah, Jeremiah, and Ezekiel followed suit. In the Song of Songs, this intimacy took the form of searching for the Beloved, finding him, and then belonging to him. In the intimacy of the mystical marriage, we are introduced to a growing love relationship between God and each person who belongs to God.

In the rooms of the fifth dwelling, the prayer of union is like a meeting between lovers that lasts for a time but is not yet a commitment. In the rooms of the sixth, a betrothal is made, a serious commitment to surrender to love. "The soul desires to be completely occupied in love and does not want to be taken up with anything else" (IC VI.7.8), and God promises the soul perfect union, or spiritual marriage. The intensity of God's love becomes evident in the rooms of this dwelling through its effects on the soul. In the seventh dwelling, the union is complete.

Teresa discovered that in the rooms of this seventh dwelling, "the Most Blessed Trinity, all three Persons, through an intellectual vision, is revealed" (IC VII.1.6). She found her home here, at the center of the soul where God dwells and where there is an overwhelming awareness of the indwelling of the Trinity. Teresa, grasping for words, came up short in her attempt to explain these Persons who have taken up residence and "never seem to leave it any more" (VII.1.7).

Does this mean that a person is so absorbed in God that she can do nothing else? Absolutely not, Teresa replies; in fact, the person is even more involved in service. Only now, she adds, she has truly enjoyable company.

As Teresa went about her daily activities and coped with suffering and setbacks toward the end of her life, she discovered that "despite the trials she underwent and the business affairs she had to attend to, that the essential part of her soul never moved from that [inner] room" (IC VII.1.10). She felt divided in two. One part of her was Martha, and the other, Mary. She complained that while Mary was immersed in quiet and peace, Martha had to accept the responsibility of handling the difficulties and disturbances of daily life.

Of course, Teresa knew that the soul is one and not split. She clarified the situation by distinguishing between spirit and soul. The "spirit" is the deepest aspect of the soul where it enjoys ongoing union with God. It is so grounded in God, says Teresa, that nothing can disturb its peace and joy. She expresses this point in a poem:

A soul, hidden away in God,
what does it need to want
but to love and love some more,
and all inflamed in love,
go back and love again? (P 15)

The "soul," however, continues to deal with the give-and-take of daily life. The result is that with the transformation that occurs in the rooms of the seventh dwelling, the person becomes both Mary and Martha, a true contemplative in action. Suffering may not diminish and struggles will remain, but the deep peace of the spirit overflows into decisions that lead to action. The person, driven to share the deep love that she has found, makes every effort to extend it to others. In effect, her will is aligned with God's and her life has become a living prayer.

"This is the reason for prayer, . . . the purpose of this spiritual marriage: the birth always of good works, good works" (IC VII.4.6), Teresa declares. The person in this final stage of the journey is certain of the divine life within her and has an overwhelming desire to serve God in all things—even wishing for a longer life to serve God more fully.

As might be expected, Teresa experienced great difficulty describing the communication and joy of union in this dwelling. In a way that was mysterious and hidden, Christ became a resident at the center of her soul, where no evil could enter. What could she say about this intimate union in which God had been communicating secretly with her all along? Teresa described her experience with poetic images like two wax candles becoming one flame, or rain falling into a stream to join with the flow of water. One thing is evident, however: in the words of St. Paul, Teresa knew with certainty that "it is no longer I, but Christ living in me" (Galatians 2:20).

We cannot appreciate Teresa's experience unless we can accept it as one of grace and great joy. The contemplative life, for Teresa, was a gift that elicited not a burdened spirit but ecstasy and celebration. She did not hide behind her words or filter her experience through abstractions, and we may have difficulty accepting her passionate love for God. Like John of the Cross, she preferred the description of lovers found in the Song of Songs. Lovers know both suffering and joy; they speak with sighs and heartfelt longing. The Song of Songs begins, "Let him kiss me with the kisses of his mouth" (1:2). Teresa wrote in one of her poems,

Oh, what a fortunate lot
was prepared for you,
for God wants you for His lover,
and has won you with His death! (P 91)

Teresa knows that waiting in silence prepares her for the divine Lover, but the initiative comes from the Beloved. God seeks her out; the Lover beyond all others is God. The unfolding story of this great love goes to the heart of Teresa's journey and ours.

The journey into the interior castle has cut through some rough terrain but now reaches an open field with a clear sky and an infinite horizon, where the soul finds its home in God. It is here where the little butterfly dies and finds its greatest freedom in Christ.

The union that Teresa experienced reminds us of the depth of meaning yet to be uncovered in our lives, especially when we are struggling to trust that we are making progress at all. It also assures us of the fundamental reality of divine love, which supports us throughout our journey. Hungering to grow in this love is the central necessity for our journey.

> In sum, . . . we shouldn't build castles in the air. The Lord doesn't look so much at the greatness of our works as at the love with which they are done. And if we do what we can, His Majesty will enable us each day to do more and more, provided that we do not quickly tire. But during the little while this life lasts—and perhaps it will last a shorter time than each one thinks—let us offer the Lord interiorly and exteriorly the sacrifice we can. (IC VII.4.15)

SUGGESTIONS FOR REFLECTION

1. For Teresa, union with God means conformity to God's will. This union is expressed in prayer but also in relationships with others. In what ways has your prayer life intensified your generous service to others?

2. According to Teresa, the true test for love of God can be found in the way we treat others. Take time to consider individual relationships and how each one of them is a sign of your closeness or your distance to divine love.

3. In her night of faith, Teresa doubted whether God truly was at the center of the castle. Did you ever question whether

you actually loved God, or whether your effort to draw close to God amounted to anything? How did these doubts affect you, and how did you regain your trust in God's call?

4. Throughout her life, Teresa valued the support of friendships and community life as a support to her prayer life. Reflect on how certain friendships and your ties to particular communities have enhanced your own prayer life.

5. Teresa's very intimacy with God made her deeply aware of her distance to divine love, and this caused her great pain. Consider how your love for God has intensified your own self-knowledge and the suffering this may have caused you.

Chapter Six

Enter and Take a Walk

I think it will be a consolation for you to delight in this interior castle since . . . you can enter and take a walk through it at any time. . . . Although no more than seven dwelling places were discussed, in each of these there are many others, below and above and to the sides, with lovely gardens and fountains and labyrinths, such delightful things.

—The Interior Castle, Epilogue, 3

Now that we have reached the center of Teresa's castle—the goal of Christian prayer—let us take seriously Teresa's invitation to turn inward and take a walk on the path at any time. How important it is to cultivate an attitude of heart and a quality of presence, and to desire to live in that presence more fully and continually. Following the path inward is not something we do but a way of honoring an experience of the divine that has been awakened in us.

Looking back at our journey, we may have gained a different perspective than the one we had when we began. Exploring the rooms of individual dwellings may have narrowed our vision, but now we are able to see the whole picture. All the dwellings seem to interlock, forming one unfolding process of growth, with each dwelling containing its unique grace and preparing us for the one ahead. Teresa encourages this view because she suggests that we enter the dwellings in order to facilitate the growth of self-knowledge: "It is good, indeed very good, to try to enter first into the room where self-knowledge is dealt with rather than fly off to other rooms" (IC I.2.9).

In addition, as we followed the path inward, we may have thought of the dwellings as stages to pass through as quickly as possible. However, for Teresa, the rooms of each dwelling introduce a vast world consisting of gardens, secret chambers, expansive spaces, and numerous surprises like fountains and hidden paths. In other words, the rooms unfold like an accordion, invoking an extraordinary spaciousness in which a soul can truly grow.

All seven dwellings together are like a labyrinth, with open-ended boundaries, multifaceted spaces, and unpredictable, serpentine paths. We soon realize that the path of prayer can reveal itself in many ways when we release our control and allow God to reveal himself anew. Contemplation, for example, can involve the practice of simple breathing in God's presence, or it can occur as we silently employ a sacred word to express our intention to remain in his presence. In fact, any time we touch our true selves and God's presence becomes apparent to us, we experience contemplation. Through her imaginative description of the dwellings, Teresa encourages us to remain alert and keep our hearts open and responsive to wherever the Spirit may lead us on the path of prayer.

Like a labyrinthine path, the castle path tends to be more cyclic than linear. We sometimes retrace our steps in order to make progress or discover that a detour takes us closer to the center. As Teresa suggests, we may even find ourselves back at the beginning because we are still struggling with the pull of worldly attractions, though all the while recognizing that these will not fulfill us.

Seen as a whole, the path through the interior castle is not a methodical progression from one state to another, but a graced adventure where anything can occur and where backtracking can be a way forward and ways of prayer can surprise us. Teresa invites us to release our adult self-consciousness and scan the rooms with the eyes of a child. Don't hold back, she says; give yourself over fully to an exploration of the castle. See your prayer life as something dynamic, not static. Live with an openness toward the indwelling presence of the Trinity, and let the thread of love draw you beneath the surface of reality to the world in God and God in the world.

In the end, Teresa promises that finding a home in the castle will mean rest and peace in our crazy lives, no matter how busy we are: "Once you get used to enjoying this castle, you will find rest in all things, even those involving much labor, for you will have the hope of returning to the castle which no one can take from you" (IC Epilogue, 2).

The Graciousness of God

In His goodness He has held me by His hand so that I might not turn back. Nor does it seem to me that I do hardly anything on my part—and that is true; I understand clearly that it is the Lord who does everything. (The Book of Her Life, 21.11)

One of the great revelations of the inner path for those who take the journey inward seriously is that everything is grace. Walking in the dark at first, we recognize eventually that we cannot escape the ever-present reality of God's light and love in our lives—namely, grace. Be assured, Teresa tells us; God is holding your hand as you walk, and "it is the Lord who does everything."

How does this grace reveal itself? Perhaps, at some point in our lives, our hearts become softer and more pliable, and we set out on a journey, willing to make a serious effort to uncover our deepest love. This journey is no walk in the park because, as Teresa warns us, "there are many who begin, yet they never reach the end. I believe this is due mainly to a failure to embrace the cross from the beginning" (BL 11.15). We see from the example of Teresa's life that embracing the cross and learning to surrender will only be possible if we open our hearts again and again to divine mercy and love.

God offers us a great deal of leeway, always coaxing and inviting, but never overriding our free will. We are loved unconditionally, but we may find ourselves incapable of responding to such generosity. Teresa describes a God "who gives so much" (BL 39.6), leaving us dumbfounded in the face of such generosity. However, even when we are slow to respond, God does not withhold his love but continues to invite us, working through our human limitations.

As years pass by, we begin to realize that the journey itself, at every turn, is completely dependent on grace. Our path is fundamentally a symphony of grace, and we discover its rhythm playing out in our bones and sinews. Ordinary life has become the raw material for our transformation, and our human limitations are molded into a graced life. Teresa understands this: "All things were a means of my knowing and loving God more, for seeing what I owed Him, and for regretting what I had been" (BL 21.10).

Grace surprises us because it transforms our life journey in ways that we once thought impossible. The map we depended on now becomes useless as we find ourselves wandering through strange terrain. We may be led along hidden alleyways and unmarked roads and through overgrown vegetation. At times we find ourselves having to make a detour, and we may even become totally lost, only to realize that we are being taught to put our lives entirely into God's hands, to trust that the Spirit will take us where we need to be.

Recall that Teresa discovered early on that her life's work would be to establish convents in which her sisters could lead a life according to the primitive spirit of the Carmelite rule. At first she was hesitant about the idea because she was comfortable at the Monastery of the Incarnation, and she knew the troubles she would face embarking on such an unpredictable adventure. However, the inner voice was persistent and would not release her, so she followed through on the practical arrangements, working hard to establish her first convent, which would be called St. Joseph's. Her journey would continue amid many twists and turns.

Teresa shows us that God waits patiently at the center of our lives, always with an eye on the path, hoping to see us rounding a corner. God listens for our familiar footsteps with arms extended to embrace us. Teresa assures us that there is abundant grace for the journey; it is up to us to respond since "he first loved us" (1 John 4:19).

Walking along This Path of Prayer Today

People must walk along this path in freedom, placing themselves in the hands of God. (The Book of Her Life, 22.12)

If we were to question Teresa about relating her path of prayer to our needs today, what would she say? How does Teresa help us—given our distance from her culture—to discover a way of praying that originates in the heart?

According to Teresa, prayer requires one fundamental practice: that we live with an open mind and heart. How else do we listen to the inner voice that calls us to deepening love? In our culture, this voice is drowned out by hyperactivity, loud noise, and ever-present diversions, leaving our minds and hearts confused and easily pulled in every direction.

Drawing on her own experience with distractions, Teresa assures us that even with the obstacles in our daily lives that make it difficult to pray or to be open to contemplation, we have the capacity to develop a listening heart. However, we need to carve out time for quiet and be willing to place our full trust in the longing of our heart for God. These times for solitude and silence may be difficult to find for a person busy with a job and the obligations of family life; for students trying to juggle assignments, papers, and tests; for those struggling to put food on the table. But Teresa insists that we need to persevere. If we make small choices each day to turn to God, who is always present and waiting to break into our hearts, then we are creating space for the indwelling of the Holy Spirit.

Even more problematic, says Teresa, is that in our time of solitude, we may encounter minds like "wild horses" (WP 19.2) that make us so restless and distracted that we are tempted to give up. Again, she counsels perseverance and returning to the presence of the Spirit of God and listening attentively. In time we will become free for God in a culture that has little patience for solitude and silence and little interest in the human capacity for God.

Teresa also offers guidance for those who are confused about the relationship between meditation and contemplation and those who sense a call to a more silent prayer. For her, as well as for John of the Cross, meditation is oriented toward contemplation and is intimately related to it. They are two features in a life dedicated to living in the presence of God. For Teresa, meditation is the prayer of active recollection and is anchored in the trust that God lives in us. Teresa believed that the humanity of Christ was integral to all forms of prayer. To pray means that throughout the day, we recall a mystery from Christ's life as a way of grounding ourselves in him. This practice of remembering Christ and identifying with an event from his life (preferably one that mirrors our own circumstances), along with growth in self-knowledge and detachment, opens our hearts to the grace of contemplation—namely, the immediate intuition of God's loving presence in our lives. Whereas meditation brings with it an inner peace and happiness, mystical prayer or contemplation offers joy beyond anything that human effort and grace can achieve.

Perhaps most important for our own active and complicated lives today, Teresa shows us that we can be contemplatives in the midst of activity. For Teresa, there is no dichotomy between action and contemplation, no need to withdraw into ideal circumstances to experience the inflow of God's love. Though the experience of prayer culminates in contemplation, gifting us with a heightened capacity to know and love God, it is not the end of the path. A person who is in love with God has the responsibility to love others in whatever way he or she is called. Action and contemplation may be distinct, but they rise up from the same inner wellspring. Teresa experienced this truth even at the end of her life when, although she experienced the constant presence of the Trinity, she was at the same time caught up in responsibilities of living in an uncertain world and had little time for prayer and reflection. In the end, for Teresa, the test for any growth in meditation and contemplation is growth in love of neighbor, which is, at the same time, a sign that one loves God.

THE ART OF A CONTEMPLATIVE WALK

People must walk along this path in freedom,
placing themselves in the hands of God.
(Book of Her Life, 22.12))

Now I invite you, using Teresa as your guide, to take a metaphorical walk inward to reinforce your life journey toward deeper union with God. We will use as touchstones for this reflection both Teresa's stages as well as the classical stages of the mystical path—purgation, illumination, and union. Teresa valued stages because she wanted us to learn the lessons that each stage has to offer. But she also appreciated that using stages to outline the spiritual path has its limitations. Because God's grace is primary, each stage can be interrupted without warning, like a sudden shift in a spring breeze, leaving the soul refreshed with an experience of love that was always present but only at that moment revealed.

We begin the walk by taking time to appreciate and give thanks for our unique personal history. At some point, we may discover that our personal history fades into the background, but for now we honor the choices we have made in the past and the choices we continue to make.

As beginners, we take our time, walking at our own pace and stopping at times to reflect on a particular attachment and the inner tug we feel to relinquish it. We also take the time to recall life events—the death of a loved one, the loss of a job, the breakup of a friendship, an illness or physical handicap—that have brought us face-to-face with our human limitations. Then we take a moment to review one of these events that holds our attention and ask ourselves how that loss has led us to change.

Consider that you are walking with others—companions on the journey, soul friends who reinforce your quest for meaning and deepen your sense of inner peace. Bring these companions to mind individually; picture each of their faces and let them, as a group, calm your restlessness or uncertainty.

With this quieting of the mind, the external journey becomes more inward and more demanding than we might have expected. We have a sense that we are in a personal relationship with God and that our entire being is at stake. Continuing along this path will mean moving deeper into the mystery of divine love. Encountering the God who is Truth, we are invited to leave behind our old lives and live according to a "new law." This new law involves a change in consciousness, not a substitution of more laws and responsibilities for the ones we already have. Then we ask ourselves, "Do I want to be completely free or not?" Our answer to this question does not come from outside of us, with the threat of punishment or the promise of reward, but from an inner imperative—from God who is the source of our inner freedom.

As we continue our walk, the inconsistencies and falsehoods of our lives become clearer, and we see ourselves as God sees us. As Teresa puts it, "All things were a means for my knowing and loving God more, for seeing what I owed Him, and for regretting what I had been" (BL 21.10). As difficult and as uncomfortable as this is, we continue to gain self-knowledge. We see the reality of our lives through God's eyes and understand something of the ugliness and painfulness of our past actions. These truths are devastating, but hope strengthens our spirit.

From the depths of the heart, we witness how God looks at us, passionately and with unconditional love. The weight of our sin does not diminish this love. In God's eyes we accept our reality, and a new love of self arises from the ashes of the old, a self-love and self-awareness formed by God.

This first movement inward involves releasing control and learning to surrender to the truth within us. It is meant to calm the mind and free up the spirit. It focuses on Teresa's question: "Can there be an evil greater than that of being ill at ease in our own house? What hope can we have of finding rest outside of ourselves if we cannot be at rest within" (IC II.1.9).

The second stage of the journey, illumination, is a time of greater clarity, of being fully present in one's life; it represents the fourth dwelling of the interior castle.

For Teresa, the transition between the third and fourth mansions is a movement from praying to God as an object distant from us to the experience of finding that God is already near, the One who prays within us. It is a movement beyond the faith of the first half of our lives—a faith in which we try to please a distant God through our actions—to a more mature faith that uncovers an intimacy with the divine within us and desires to live always in this presence.

At this stage, the walk begins to take on a life of its own. The gift of each moment is enough to satisfy us. Aware of a hidden center of love calling to us, we feel a distance toward the business of life. Concerns that were once weighing on us no longer seem as important; an appetite for things mundane and trivial lessens. Perhaps a brief moment of self-forgetfulness and immersion in the divine presence takes us by surprise and leaves wonder and awe in its wake.

As we walk, we become aware that prayer is less and less tied to words and images but rather is a silent participation in the prayer of Christ. Our deepest desire is that when we say "I," we mean "Christ." "It is no longer I, but Christ living in me" (Galatians 2:20). We pray for the grace to see others and the world through Christ's eyes, the eyes of compassion, love, awareness, and sacrifice. We realize that becoming ourselves means becoming "clothed in Christ" (Galatians 3:27).

Following Teresa's counsel, we release our control as we continue to journey and let divine initiative and action take over. We become more at home in silence and develop an attitude of waiting. This is difficult because we want to know that we are progressing, but we need to renounce all desire for results. Making the walk successful should not be our concern; our willingness to walk in silence and let the silence deepen into mystery is enough.

Sometimes we catch a hint of divine presence when we least expect it. For example, we recall a time when God's grace was evident, overflowing the limitations of our experience. These moments of encounter offer consolation, but they are primarily a challenge to open the door of the heart more fully to humility and love. For the most part, we may feel no warm feelings but only dryness; however, we appreciate that this is an invitation from God to a more simple prayer. If we respond with naked faith, a relationship evolves that bonds our will with that of God. The proof of this is, to borrow Teresa's image, an overflowing love that pours out of an inner wellspring and into the lives of others. In short, we become more loving and compassionate.

What is the seeker meant to hear and how is she to act at this time in her life? For this state of prayer, Teresa advises that

> without any effort . . . the soul should strive to cut down the rambling of the intellect . . . ; it is good to be aware that one is in God's presence and of who God is. . . . Let it not strive to understand the nature of this recollection . . . [and] enjoy it without any endeavors other than some loving words. (IC IV.3.7)

The stage of union, which corresponds to final three dwellings in the interior castle, is marked by communion with the holy, losing the self in a state of oneness with God. The person stays in touch with the flame of love within herself, whether its warmth can be felt or not. If there is no sense of the divine presence, then the pilgrim finds reassurance from a past experience of being touched by divine love.

Silence becomes our prayer, but as Teresa warns, the practice of silence will never be an attempt to remain in a state of blank unknowing. In the silence, we are called to greater self-knowledge and fidelity to the truth. We are called to release all the lies in our lives. Teresa is clear that there is no room for evasion in our response to God; it is emotionally honest, or it is nothing.

This flame of love grounds us in the truth of who we are, the person God calls us to be, and charges us with the energy to share our gifts with others. The pilgrim's focus now turns outward. We continue to ask, "In what way do I feel empowered? How am I called to integrate my authentic self into the world after experiencing God's nearness?" Teresa provides this answer:

You may think that as a result the soul will be . . . so absorbed that it will be unable to be occupied with anything else. On the contrary, the soul is much more occupied than before with everything pertaining to the service of God; and once its duties are over it remains with that enjoyable company. If the soul does not fail God, He will never fail . . . to make His presence clearly known to it. (IC VII.1.8)

THE JOURNEY INTO PRAYER: CULMINATION

For Teresa, contemplative prayer is the goal for all Christians. Today many ache for a prayer that is more and more simple, that can become deeply imbedded in their hearts, and that can continue to feed and heal their spirits throughout their daily routine. Teresa takes us by the hand and walks with us toward the discovery of this prayer. She offers us a primal awareness of God in which the mind deals less with thoughts and ideas and the heart is invited to release itself from its bonds.

Fundamentally, Teresa teaches us that at the center of each believer's heart there exists an intimate relationship with Christ, waiting to be uncovered. It is our longing for this relationship that drives us unknowingly to seek an ultimate answer to the question.

She believed that the humanity of Christ, once available to those who lived in Jerusalem at a certain period in time, is now present to us each moment. That's because the incarnation of the Word became part of human history; the presence of the resurrected Christ continues without limitation of space and time. Not only is Christ in heaven, but he also continues to walk with his disciples on earth. Jesus himself tells us, "Look, I am with you always; yes, to the end of time" (Matthew 28:20).

It is simple, says Teresa: through prayer we become aware of a God who is already close to us in Christ, and through prayer we develop an ongoing love relationship with Christ. In her own faithfulness to prayer, Teresa uncovered an image of Christ that at first introduced her to her radical dependence on God and later reflected her belovedness as an image of God. By gazing at Christ, Teresa uncovered her authentic self with the capacity to love others unconditionally.

Teresa is quick to remind us not to hesitate to enter the castle repeatedly, because in spite of its difficulty, the path we travel toward a deepening relationship with Christ holds the promise of boundless delight and joy. She assures us with a consoling metaphor: the heart, a sailboat being tossed dangerously by the churning waves of a wild sea, all the while remains secure and content in God.

> Happy is the heart in love . . .
> because all his intentions are toward God.
> And thus he sails happily and joyfully
> o'er the waves of this tempestuous sea. (P 17)

SUGGESTIONS FOR REFLECTION

1. Think of your entire prayer life as a rhythmic movement of grace, a dance between yourself and divine love. When along this path of grace did you feel that God was truly holding your hand and walking alongside you? Let the memory of these times open your heart to prayer.

2. How are you embracing the cross and surrendering to God's will in your prayer life now? Has this openness of heart intensified your awareness of God's unlimited mercy and love?

3. Imagine Teresa walking with you, speaking to the depths of your heart, sharing her longing for God and supporting your desire for divine love in the midst of your unique journey. What counsel does she offer you at this point in your life?

4. Take time to reflect and perhaps record in a journal any insights you may want to explore. Trust that this experience has changed your vision and strengthened your determination to follow the inner call even though you do not feel reinforced or renewed by the experience. Let faith alone be your support on this interior path of self-discovery.

Suggested Reading

Bielecki, Tessa. *Teresa of Avila: Mystical Writings*. New York: Crossroad Publishing, 1994.

_____. *Holy Daring: An Outrageous Gift to Modern Spirituality from Saint Teresa, the Grand Wild Woman of Avila*. Rockport, MA: Element Books, Ltd., 1994.

Blinkoff, Jodi. *The Avila of Saint Teresa: Religious Reform in a Sixteenth-Century City*. Ithaca, NY: Cornell University Press, 1989.

Burrows, Ruth. *Fire Upon the Earth: Interior Castle Explored*. Denville, NJ: Dimension Books, 1981.

Chorpenning, Joseph F., OSFS. *The Divine Romance: Teresa of Avila's Narrative Theology*. Chicago: Loyola University Press, 1992.

Clissold, Stephen. *St. Teresa of Avila*. New York: Seabury Press, 1982.

du Boulay, Shirley. *Teresa of Avila: An Extraordinary Life*. New York: BlueBridge, 2004.

Gross, Francis, Jr. *The Making of a Mystic: Seasons in the Life of Teresa of Avila*. Albany, NY: State University of New York Press, 1993.

John of the Cross. *The Spiritual Canticle* in *The Collected Works of St. John of the Cross*, rev. ed. Trans. by Kieran Kavanaugh, OCD and Otilio Rodriguez, OCD. Washington, DC: ICS Publications, 1979.

Luti, Mary J. *Teresa of Avila's Way*. Collegeville, MN: Liturgical Press, 1991.

May, Gerald G., MD. *The Dark Night of the Soul: A Psychiatrist Explores the Connection Between Darkness and Spiritual Growth*. New York: HarperCollins Publishers, 2004.

McGreal, Wilfrid, OCarm. At *the Fountain of Elijah: The Carmelite Tradition*. New York: Orbis Books, 1999.

Medwick, Cathleen. *Teresa of Avila: The Progress of a Soul*. New York: Alfred A. Knopf, 1999.

Mujica, Barbara. *Teresa de Avila: Lettered Woman*. Nashville: Vanderbilt University Press, 2009.

O'Donoghue, Noel. *Mystics for Our Time: Carmelite Meditations for a New Age*. Collegeville, MN: Liturgical Press, 1989.

_____. *Adventures in Prayer: Reflections on St. Teresa of Avila, St. John of the Cross, and St. Thérèse of Lisieux*. New York: Continuum, 2002.

Weber, Alison. *Teresa of Avila and the Rhetoric of Femininity*. Princeton, NJ: Princeton University Press, 1990.

Welch, John, OCarm. *Spiritual Pilgrims: Carl Jung and Teresa of Avila*. Mahwah, NJ: Paulist Press, 1982.

Endnotes

1. Kate O'Brien, *Teresa of Avila* (London: Max Parrish, 1951), 94.

2. Quoted in Shirley du Boulay, *Teresa of Avila: An Extraordinary Life* (New York: BlueBridge, 2004), 205.

3. *The Saints: Humanly Speaking*, ed. Felicitas Corrigan, OSB (Ann Arbor, MI: Servant Publications, 2000), 240.

4. *Edith Stein: Essential Writings*, ed. John Sullivan, OCD (New York: Orbis Books, 2002), 22.

5. Dorothy Day, *The Long Loneliness* (San Francisco: Harper and Row, 1952), 140–41.

6. *At the Fountain of Elijah: The Carmelite Tradition*, Wilfred McGreal, O Carm (New York: Orbis Books, 1999), 125–26.

7. Francisco de Osuna, *The Third Spiritual Alphabet*, trans. and intro. Mary E. Giles (New York: Paulist Press, 1981), 47.

8. Quoted in Shirley du Boulay, *Teresa of Avila: An Extraordinary Life*, 106.

9. Quoted in Shirley du Boulay, *Teresa of Avila: An Extraordinary Life*, 265.

10. *The Confessions of St. Augustine*, trans. John K. Ryan (New York: Image Books, 1960), 254.

11. Thomas Merton, *The Wisdom of the Desert* (New York: New Directions Publishing, 1960), 11.

12. *Cries of the Spirit: A Celebration of Women's Spirituality*, ed. Marilyn Sewell (Boston: Beacon Press, 1991), 259.

13. *Aging as a Spiritual Journey*, Eugene C. Bianchi (New York: Crossroad Publishing, 1995), 122.

14. Antoine de Saint Exupéry, *The Little Prince* (New York: Harcourt Brace Jovanovich Publishers, 1971), 80–84.

15. Anthony de Mello, *Sadhana: A Way to God* (New York: Image Books, 1984), 78.

16. John Welch, O Carm, *Spiritual Pilgrims: Carl Jung and Teresa of Avila* (New York: Paulist Press, 1982), 97.

17. Quoted in Shirley du Boulay, *Teresa of Avila: An Extraordinary Life*, 178.

18. Mary Margaret Funk, *Into the Depths: A Journey of Loss and Vocation* (New York: Lantern Books, 2011), 155–56.

19. Thomas Merton, *Contemplative Prayer* (New York: Image Books, 1971), 70.

20. *The Confessions of St. Augustine*, trans. John K. Ryan, 254.

21. Wayne Simsic, *Faith: Daily Prayers for Virtue* (Winona, MN: St. Mary's Press, 1997), 76.

22. Thomas Merton, *The Seven Storey Mountain: An Autobiography of Faith* (New York: Harcourt Brace and Company, 1998), 253.

23. Julian of Norwich, *Showings* (long text), trans. Edmund Colledge, OSA, and James Walsh, SJ (New York: Paulist Press, 1978), 273–74.

24. Fr. Earnest Larkin explains, "In this prayer [of recollection] the recall of an image from the Passion functioned in the same ways as the sacred word." *Carmelite Prayer: A Tradition for the 21st Century*, ed. Keith J. Egan (Mahwah, NJ: Paulist, 2003), 214.

25. John Shea, *Following Jesus* (New York: Orbis Books, 2010), 57.

26. Keith J. Egan in *Carmelite Prayer: A Tradition for the 21st Century*, ed. Keith J. Egan (Mahwah, NJ: Paulist Press), 50.

27. Thomas Merton, *Honorable Reader: Reflections on My Work*, ed. Robert E. Daggy (New York: Crossroad, 1991), 134.

28. Gerald G. May, MD, *The Dark Night of the Soul: A Psychiatrist Explores the Connection Between Darkness and Spiritual Growth* (New York: HarperCollins Publishers, 2004), 67.

29. Gerald G. May, MD, *The Dark Night of the Soul*, 95.

30. *The Collected Works of St. John of the Cross*, rev. ed., trans. Kieran Kavanaugh, OCD, and Otilio Rodriguez OCD (Washington, DC: ICS Publications, 1979), *The Dark Night*, I.5.3; 306.

31. *The Collected Works of St. John of the Cross*, *The Dark Night* I.7.5, 311.

32. Gerald G. May, MD, *Will and Spirit: A Contemplative Psychology* (San Francisco: Harper & Row, Publishers, 1982), 16.

33. *Spiritual Writings: Soren Kierkegaard*, trans. George Pattison (New York: HarperCollins Publishers, 2010), 185–86.

34. Denise Levertov, *The Stream & the Sapphire* (New York: New Directions Publishing, 1997), 15.

35. *The Collected Works of St. John of the Cross*, *Spiritual Canticle* 8.3, 441.

36. John Welch, O Carm, *Spiritual Pilgrims: Carl Jung and Teresa of Avila*, 137.

37. Gerald G. May, MD, *The Dark Night of the Soul*, 90.

theWORD
among us®
The *Spirit* of Catholic Living

This book was published by The Word Among Us. Since 1981, The Word Among Us has been answering the call of the Second Vatican Council to help Catholic laypeople encounter Christ in the Scriptures.

The name of our company comes from the prologue to the Gospel of John and reflects the vision and purpose of all of our publications: to be an instrument of the Spirit, whose desire is to manifest Jesus' presence in and to the children of God. In this way, we hope to contribute to the Church's ongoing mission of proclaiming the gospel to the world so that all people would know the love and mercy of our Lord and grow ever more deeply in love with him.

Our monthly devotional magazine, *The Word Among Us*, features meditations on the daily and Sunday Mass readings, and currently reaches more than one million Catholics in North America and another half million Catholics in one hundred countries around the world. Our book division, The Word Among Us Press, publishes numerous books, Bible studies, and pamphlets that help Catholics grow in their faith.

To learn more about who we are and what we publish, log on to our website at www.wau.org. There you will find a variety of Catholic resources that will help you grow in your faith.

Embrace His Word, Listen to God . . .

www.wau.org